THE COUNTRY DIARY
OF AN
EDWARDIAN
GNOME

PRIVATE EYE / ANDRE DEUTSCH

Published in Great Britain by Private Eye Productions Ltd.,
34, Greek Street, London W.1.
In association with Andre Deutsch Ltd.,
105, Great Russell Street, London W.C.1.

ISBN 233 97304 4

Printed by Billing & Sons Ltd.,
Walnut Tree Close,
Guildford, Surrey.

Designed by Peter Windett & Associates.

Storm grows over "Princess" film

by Our London Correspondent
Mohammed El Deedesh

THE ENGLISH-SPEAKING world was up in arms yesterday after last night's showing on Saudi TV of a two-hour "drama documentary" on the life of a British princess and her alleged love affair with a young welfare state scrounger forty years her junior.

I understand that the British Royal household has taken "grave offence" at the film, which shows the ageing Princess lounging on a Caribbean beach while her young lover croons French pop songs to the strains of a small ukelele.

SHOCK

A British Palace official yesterday claimed that the film was a "disgraceful attack" on the traditional beliefs of millions of Anglicans all over the world.

He pointed out that the Princess is the sister of the head of the Church of England, and therefore a person held in deep reverence by all devout Englishmen.

This view was confirmed by a leading dignitary of the Anglican Church, the Rt. Rev. "Ayatollah" Flannel, who said, "There is nothing in the Princess's long-standing 'live-in' friendship with Mr Llewellyn which is at all at odds with recent trends in Anglican teaching on meaningful one-to-one relationships within the frame-work of an extra-marital affair.

"So far from being punished for her offences as she would be in Islamic countries," the Rev. Flannel droned on, "the Princess is treated by our media in a proper spirit of Christian compassion, and she has even been given a pay rise as a token of the great esteem in which she is held by the British people."

JEDDIT?

As the row grew last night to minuscule proportions, an unrepentant Lunchtime O'Nobooze, the producer of the award-winning film, claimed that he had not intended in any way to criticise the Western way of life.

"While making 'Princess'," he said, "we spoke to more than ten million people, tape-recorded thousands of inter-views and shot over 500 miles of film. I agree that the end-product is a load of rubbish, but no one can deny that investigative journalism of this type has a vital role to play in bringing about World War Three."

Mother Esther of Lime Grove

by the Venerable Beeb

One of the most loved of all the saints in the calendar is Mother Esther, miracle-worker and friend of the poor housewife.

Although, sadly, nothing is known of Esther's early life, it is believed that she came from humble stock and that her father was a lowly but honest hairdresser in the town of Norwich.

As a young girl Esther was drawn to follow a holy man of the time, the Blessed Braden, who was best-known for the astonishing miracle whereby he persuaded millions of ordinary, pious folk to consume tins of Campbell's Soup. It was during this time of her life that Esther also fell under the spell of the man who was to become her 'teacher' and life-long friend, Father Desmond O'Wilcox, a simple Irish priest who went round the country "putting his foot in the door" to help the poor.

Soon, with Father Desmond's help, the Blessed Bernard ascended into heaven (or, as they used to put it in the quaint phrasing of the time, was 'kicked upstairs'). The young and beautiful Esther took his place, and before long her fame as a miracle-worker had spread far and wide.

Each Sunday night, she would leave her cloistered cell to 'appear' before the people, to help them in their sufferings and to guide them along the devotional path to the beatific state of 'full Consumer awareness'.

An old age pensioner in Balham was having trouble with the Gas Board. Esther interceded for her — and within ten minutes, two workmen miraculously appeared to fix her Ascot heater. A couple in Leamington sent off £50 for a course on 'How To Become A Millionaire In Two Weeks'. They got no reply. But Esther was swiftly on the trail, and the villain, a Mr Aswan Gerhardi of Lee Bank, Birmingham, was soon miraculously behind bars.

But the greatest miracle of all came late in Esther's life. One day an angel came to her and said, "Esther, blessed art thou above all women — for thou shalt bear a daughter, and her name shall be

"Mother Esther may never have existed"

Theologian's Shock Claim

by Our Religious Affairs Correspondent
CLIFFORD LONGFORD

■ According to well-known Cambridge theologian, the Rev. Don Stupitt, 'The Blessed Mother Esther' may never have been a historical figure, but simply a figment of popular legend.

Writing in the theological magazine, *The New Atheist*, the Rev. Stupitt warns that the well-loved version of Esther's life attributed to the Venerable Beeb was almost certainly the work of a number of *Radio Times* hacks who merely 'did it for a laugh'.

"There were many such figures at the time," the Rev. Stupitt goes on. "St Melvyn of Cumbria, the Blessed Angela, St James of Savile — all of whom have been shown by recent work in America to be entirely mythical personages, accredited by the credulous people of a superstitious age with supernatural powers.

"If Mother Esther did exist — and we are still waiting for the results of recent carbon-dating tests carried out by the NASA space team — then she was almost certainly a one-legged man with a ginger beard, better known as Lord Goodman — but we can never be sure."

Rev. Stupitt is 23.

called Emily Alice. And she shall be exalted. And her picture shall be on the cover of the *Radio Times.*"

And Esther was sore amazed. For she was well advanced in years, unmarried and barren.

But, lo, it came to pass even as the angel had spake. Esther gave birth. And there was rejoicing throughout the land. And old age pensioners danced with teenagers in the streets.

And Esther was held up as an example to all women, as the 'Holy Mother Esther of Lime Grove'. And wherever Esther went the baby went too, spreading happiness and joy to all who gazed upon them.

Radio 3

647kHz/464m
VHF: 90-92.5

6.55 am Weather

7.0 News

7.5 Your Midweek Choice
Listeners' record requests
Humdinger Concerto for Piano,
Cello and Flute (DF4602)
MARCEL PIGOTT-BROWN
(piano)
LUCINDA MITSUBUSHI
(Cello)
OSSIAN PRENDERGAST
(flute)
LE PETIT ORCHESTRE DE
GENEVE
Conductor: WALLINGFORD
DE LA YOGHOURT

7.14 Smirnoff: Symphonic
Poem — The Mausoleum of
Yuri the Great
GLASGOW PHILHARMONIC
ORCHESTRA
Conductor: WASIM DRIBERG

7.40 Perrier: Chanson
Grotesque

VITTORIA DE LOS BAL-
HAMAS (soprano)
GILES GORDON (piano)

8.0 News

8.5 *Stereo*
Part 2 Martini Concerto in C
Major for Six Harpsichords
I SOLISTI DI OSLO
Conductor: SIR CHARLES
MUGABE
Studebaker In Memoriam LBJ
1969
Tenor Soloist: HERCULE
LONDQVIST-RUSHTON
THE PHILIPPINES RADIO
SYMPHONY ORCHESTRA
Conductor: HITLER VON
KARAVAN
Bragg Cumbrian Rhapsody
(arr. ANTHONY HOLDEN)
THE SOUTH BANK
ORCHESTRA
Conducted by ANDREAS
PEPSICOLOS Jr.

9.0 News

9.05 Composers of the Week
Fortnum and Mason

Fortnum Lacrimae for My
Ladye Forkbender
BELSIZE PARK CONSORT
OF VIOLS
(Solo lute: RODNEY POOF-
WILKINSON)
Mason Two Dirges (1541)
SCUOLA CANTORUM DI
SASKATCHEWAN
(Conducted by ENRICO
CUDLIPP)

10.0 Organ Recital
Heineken: Praeludium in B-
Flat
Quarg: Antiphon 'Anorexia
Nervosa'
Boulanger: Requiem Triste
1971
Timpson: Epithalamion III
GODFREY TIMPSON (organ)
from the Parish Church at
Heckmondwicke.

10.30 Modern Korean Folksong
YANG CHANG-TUN (obla)
and WING FAN-DUK (strob).
Introduced by YEHUDI
BOYDEN

11.0 Test Match Special

*"Mr Thragford has been interested in trans-
vestism from the word go"*

Some people demolish

demolish

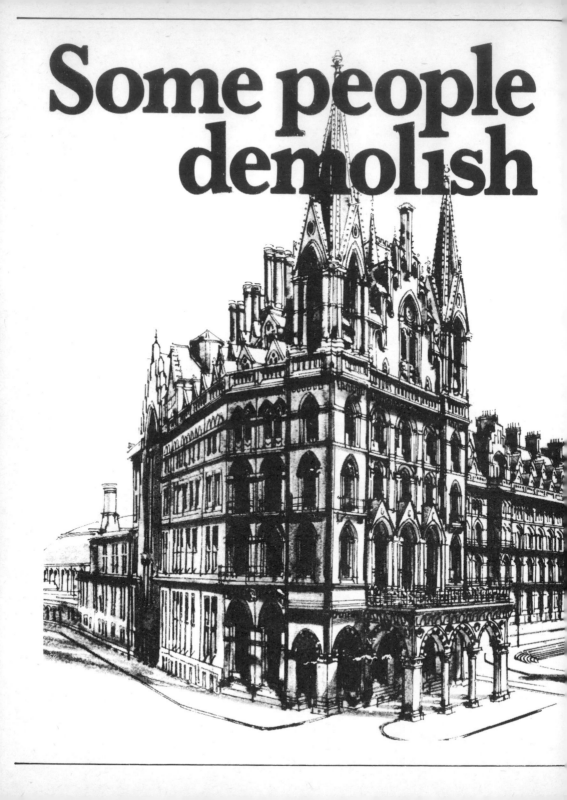

would it.

In fact, that's just what British Rail wanted to do ten years ago.

Only they weren't allowed to, by the GLC Historic Buildings Board.

Apparently a lot of long-haired sentimentalists like Sir John Betjeman thought there was something special about this horrible, tatty old Victorian pile.

Even now, if we wanted to knock it down, these faceless bureaucrats wouldn't let us.

In fact we've got hundreds of these ghastly old relics dotted about the country.

We've been trying to knock most of them down and sell them to property speculators for years.

In some cases we even managed to slip it through — look at those wonderful new office blocks that Richard Seifert has put up where the Euston Arch used to stand.

But as for the rest of all this so-called architectural heritage — we're lumbered with it.

So we've decided to do the next best thing, by spending thousands of pounds taking ludicrous advertisements all over the place, claiming that we care passionately about these wonderful gems of British culture — in the hope that a few idiots might be gulled into thinking that Sir Peter Parker is a deeply sensitive figure, similar to Lord Clark of Civilisation.

Only to be used in case of emergency

TO THE EDITOR OF THE DAILY TELEGRAPH

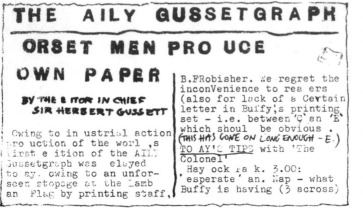

THE AILY GUSSETGRAPH

ORSET MEN PRO UCE

OWN PAPER

BY THE E ITOR IN CHIEF
SIR HERBERT GUSSETT

Owing to in ustrial action
pro uction of the worl ,s
first e ition of the AILY
Gussetgraph was elayed
to ay. owing to an unfor-
seen stopage at the Lamb
an Flag by printing staff,

B.FRobisher. We regret the
inconVenience to rea ers
(also for lack of a Certain
letter in Buffy's printing
set - i.e. between 'G' an 'E'
which shoul be obvious .
(THIS HAS GONE ON LONG ENOUGH - E.)
TO AY'S TIPS with 'The
Colonel'
. Hay ock ra k. 3.00:
'esperate' an. Nap - what
Buffy is having (3 across)

From Sir Herbert Gussett

DEAR SIR (if you are still
there)—This letter may never
reach you. For all I know you
and your gallant staff have
already been massacred by the
Marxist-trained SOGAT
guerillas who we learn have
taken over your wonderful
newspaper and all that it
stands for.

But I would like you to
know how a little handful of
us, out here in a remote corner
of the West Country, are
coping with the greatest crisis
our civilisation has ever faced.
Let me say at once that it has
not been an easy time for any
of us. Perhaps no one will ever
come through from these grim
days to light once again the
beacon which, you will
remember, resulted in the loss
of the following items during
the late Jubilee Celebrations:

1 wife *(slightly foxed)*
1 Fox *(slightly stuffed)*
1 collection cigarette cards
('Great Golfers' — two missing
from set)

1 Windsor Chintz Armchair
(formerly property of the
Wheatcroft Arms Hotel,
Bexhill)
1 house *(slightly thatched)*
etc. etc.
But I digress.
When we heard the news
from the BBC that these
terrorists had taken charge of
the dear old *Telegraph*, I can
tell you we prepared for a long
siege. An *ad hoc* Committee
was formed of loyal readers in
this area, consisting of the
following:
Chairman, Treasurer and
Editor-in-Chief: H. GUSSETT.
Secretary, News Editor and
Racing Tipster: B. FRO-
BISHER.
Girl Friday etc: LETITIA
GUSSETT (my wife).
Our plan was simple. To
print each day our own edition
of the finest newspaper in the
world and thus to keep the
flag flying in at least one neck
of the woods — viz. Loose
Chippings, the village in which
we have the honour to live.

Fortunately, Buffy had in
his possession the one sine-
qua-non of producing one's
own newspaper — to wit, a
John Bull Printing Set, pre-
sented to him by a kindly
uncle on the occasion of his
9th Birthday (many years ago
now!).
Obviously we could not
hope, Sir, to emulate your
own magnificent organ in every
detail. Nevertheless, we went
to work with a will, and before
too many days were out, we
were holding in our hands, hot
off the presses, the first
edition of the *Daily Gussettgraph*. (We had decided for
libel reasons that it would be
inadvisable to call our paper
by your own illustrious name,
but we had chosen the nearest
suitable equivalent.)
Although our edition was
not very long (it only con-
sisted, alas, of one rather
small sheet, slightly smudged),
the enclosed facsimile of the
contents will be enough for
you and your readers to judge
how well we fared against all
the many obstacles that con-
fronted us.
I leave the world to judge
of our achievement.
Let it never be said that in
Britain's hour of need we
shirked our duty.
I remain, Sir, your obedient
servant,

H. GUSSETT
Proprietor and
Editor-in-Chief
The Daily Gussettgraph
Lower Case, Beds.

GNOME HOUSE FORTE PRESENT

SITUATED ONLY FOUR MILES FROM BISHOP'S
STORTFORD IN DELIGHTFUL HERTS COUNTRYSIDE

NEW

GULAG G.B.

Britain's first Russian-style Labour Camp where you can rediscover the real YOU in conditions of supreme discomfort.

For only £850 a week you can experience a Solzhenitsyn-style rebirth of the type hitherto only available in the Soviet Union.

WHAT WILL I GET WHEN I VISIT GULAG GB?

Nothing to eat
Torture
Midnight interrogation
No toilet facilities
+ complete spiritual rejuvenation.

Jungian expert Dr Magnus Booker, psychiatric adviser to Gulag House Forte, writes: *"Man is born twice. The first time in an every-day sense — The second in the truly enriching environment of total deprivation. Trust House Gulag says more about you than cash ever can. I cannot recommend it too highly."*

Send for our specially censored brochure to GNOME HOUSE FORTE LTD., PO Box 94, Coren House, Leicester.

The Secret Life of

JACKIE KENNEDY

By Glenda Slagburger and Rhoda Koenig

For years the world has been fed on an all-too-familiar picture of President Kennedy and his wife Jackie as the least well-suited couple of modern times.

How often have we been told about the 'other women' in Jack's life? Or the story of how old Joe Kennedy paid Jackie millions of dollars to keep up the pretence of a happy marriage?

We've heard until we've been bored to death of Jackie's tantrums, of her alleged refusals to appear at State banquets, of her absurd love of clothes and money.

We can now reveal that the reality was very different. Behind the all-American facade of a couple constantly on the brink of divorce, the truth is that in fact Jack and Jackie were blissfully in love. Every night Jackie would wait patiently for her husband to get back from the White House where he worked, warming his slippers by the fire.

"Ah, Jack," she would declare, as the doorbell chime played a snatch from their favourite musical, *Camelot*, "ah'm mighty glad to see you. You'll never guess what ah've prepared for yoh dinner tonight, honey."

Jack would look puzzled for a moment, and then his handsome face would pucker with pleasure at the delicious aroma issuing from the kitchen.

"Well, I'll be darned," the tanned, athletic ex-Pacific naval hero would exclaim. "That smells to me jus' like you've been re-heatin' one of our very good friend Col. Sanders' delicious but tasteless Special Kosher Fried Chicken Dinners." *(Contd. for next four weeks.)*

Trelford-Trash Productions Inc.

"He says he's filling the gap left by John Wayne"

Bernard Levin

(age 53.7.)

What I did in the summer holidays

My best day in the summer holidays was when I went to a big art gallery in France.

I saw a lot of famous paintings which are famous. They are by Cezanne, Leonardo da Vinci, Monet and some artists called The Impressionists. The pictures were very nice.

Afterwards I went to a fantastic restaurant called *Les Trois Pigeons Qui Chantent Dans Le Bois*. This is what I had for lunch: two *douzaines* of Escargots St. Germaine Greer en Beurre Noire; a Fricasee de Canards aux Ecrevisses Flambees en Grand Marnier, avec Chocolate Sauce; then Poulet Roti Arabien Duc de Gloucester a la Colonel Sanders de Kentucky, with Pommes Frites Dauphinoise and Haricots Toadthrush garni with watercress, truffles etc. And for pudding I had Les Grandes Profiterolles de Limoges in jam sauce, with Fruits de Saison, Glaces, Fromage etc.

To drink, I had a bottle of Chateau Jacques Loussier 1947, then a bottle of Katzenellenbogen Cabinett Trockenbeeren Auslese 1955, then a bottle of Chateau Etwindus 1924, washed down with liqueurs, brandy and coffee.

In the afternoon I had a little nap. In the evening I went to Wagner's *Der Matterhorn* at the Opera House. It was very nice.

Afterwards I had dinner at the *Le Petit Cottage de Milord Bradwell*. I started with three Douzaines of Langoustes Enormes Balon avec Grapefruit Segments
(Contd. p 94)

COGGAN'S HOPES FOR INTERCOMMUNION RISE AS NEW POPE LOOMS

by **CLIFFORD LONGFORD**,
Our Religious Affairs Correspondent

"I've got squatters"

"Whoever is chosen as the new Pope, I sincerely hope that he will have intercommunion with me as soon as possible."

These were the historic words spoken last night by the Rt. Rev. Donald Duck, Archbishop of Canterbury.

Dr Duck, who for long has been an impassioned and outspoken advocate of intercommunion at any price, denied rumours that the 'women priests' row at present rocking the Anglican Communion to its foundations would prove an obstacle to "this momentous step forward".

Last night the Anglican Communion was rocked to its foundations when a West Indian steel band held a Reggae-Bozanquet-Style Interdenominational Stomp-In in front of the High Altar of Canterbury Cathedral.

Thousands of bejeaned bishops frugged and twisted the night away as part of what Dr Duck described as "a meaningful effort to bring the Church into line with the needs of the Third World, and an ongoing pastoral-outreach-situation more relevant to the lives of the average teenager-in-the-pew."

Dr Duck is 91.

"And here's Sharon, two weeks after she was conceived"

As told to Malcolm Muggerishkyn

A LIFE IN THE DAY OF

GOD

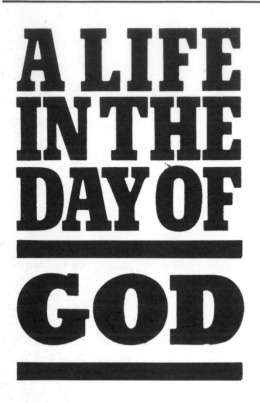

"Staying awake as I do all the time, I have always found it very difficult to go to sleep. Nevertheless, when I get up, the first thing I like to do is to read *The Times*. I turn at once to the obituaries, to see who I should be expecting for lunch. Last week, for instance, I had Pope Paul VI, Victor Sylvester and Doris Waters, a lively lady who kept us all amused with her tales of a life spent in what I gather is called show-business.

After breakfast, I potter down into my study, a modest little room occupying only four galaxies, and constructed of onyx, chalcedony and some agreeable little white clouds designed by Signor Tiepolo. I cannot wait to hear what Lord Clark has to say about them when he gets up here — if he does!

I spend the morning listening to messages that have been left overnight on the Ansaphone — mainly appeals for guidance, help and so forth. Thank Myself, there are less of these than there used to be. I am told that I don't have quite the following I used to have!

Someone once said that I move 'in a mysterious way'. I have always thought that of all the many things that have been said of me, this is one of the more percipient!

I have never bothered with food, so at lunchtime I just look in on my latest batch of guests to see how they are faring. Today there are only seven of them — I gather that none of the other 27,562,421 applicants were accepted.

Now it is time for me to have my daily visit from the gifted team who are working on plans for my next production — the so-called Day of Judgement. Signor Michelangelo shows me some rough sketches for the opening scenes, when mountains dissolve, oceans boil over and that sort of thing. I am not sure that the background music by Signor Verdi is quite tasteful enough — all that brass! But I have taken quite a shine to a funny little American with a cigar called De Mille, who wanders around saying, "Jeez, this is just like the way I thought it would look."

All in all, it is a pretty lonely business up here, and I sometimes wonder whether it's all worth it. But I like to think I do some good in the world, just by being here.

NEXT WEEK: Mary Quant.

THE INTERVIEW THAT SHOCKED THE NATION

At last – in full – why Edward Heath will never captain Yorkshire again

As told to MICHAEL BARGINSON

BARGINSON: T'good evening. It is my very special privilege to welcome tonight t'man who has been described as "T'greatest living Yorkshireman in t'world" (©Harold Wislon). I mean of course Geoff Borecott.

(Enter slight, balding man in England cricket cap. He steps over prostrate figure of Barginson and sits down.)

BORECOTT: You can get up off your knees now, Mike.

BARGINSON: Geoff, you and I have been old muckers ever since we used to play cricket together up against t'wall of tripe factory in Barnsley (©J.B. Priestley).

BORECOTT: Oh, aye. 'appen I don't remember (©H. Evans).

BARGINSON: Geoff, the question the whole world is waiting for an answer to tonight is — why 'ave t'daft boogers at t'Yorkshire Cricket Club got it in for thee? (©D.H. Lawrence).

BORECOTT: Aye. These bloody Southerners are all t'same. They don't know owt about nowt. *(Begins to weep.)* Tell me this, Mike — what have I done wrong? I'm only a simple opening bat who's made more runs than anyone else in t'history of t'game. Did you know that last year alone I had 37 innings, 7 not out, I made 4,819 runs. . .

BARGINSON: Wonderful. I think the hand-picked audience would like a chance to applaud the greatest batsman in t'history of t'world. . .

(Assembled members of Borecott fan club cheer hysterically.)

BARGINSON: In addition, you are, are you not, a very beguiling and charming person in your own right (©Russell Bargy)?

BORECOTT: 'appen I am. I don't want to be personal but what 'as that daft booger Brearley ever done to deserve t'captaincy? 'E just stands there in his bloody daft motor-cycle hat, whistling t'bloody stuck-up music like. . .

BARGINSON: Terrifig (©M. Barg and D. Frosd)!

BORECOTT: But I'll tell thee this lad. What it all boils down to is loyalty. That's t'only thing that matters. I'm the only one left who knows what t'word means.

(Renews weeping. Barginson weeps. Audience fidgets uncomfortably. Soft string music swells to climax. Gulls mew. Picture cuts to Yorkshire moor, where man in cricket blazer and flannels is walking dog.)

DEEP MASCULINE VOICE OVER: Loyalty — the one thing money can't buy.

(Dog bites man in leg. Man kicks dog.)

FADES

©Dametrash TV Spectaculars 1978

NUCLEAR ATTACK NO MORE LIKELY THAN BEE STING

ABSURD PEER'S SHOCK CLAIM

by Our TV Correspondent
Derek and Clive-James-Herriott

In last night's Dimblebore Lecture, the former head of the Government's sperm-bank, Lord Rothschild, lashed out at Britain's bee-keepers.

"Statistics show", he said, "that since 1945 18,000,000% more people have been killed by accidents involving bees than have died in nuclear holocausts."

Lord Rothschild then unveiled a gigantic graph showing the figures for fatalities under these headings:

RISK FATALITY SITUATIONS	
Bee-Stings	
	1 in 56,000,000 (the late Mrs Ethel Weems)
Nuclear Holocausts	
	NIL
1945	1974

© *Dr J. Miller*

"So much", proclaimed the balding peer, "for the moaning Minnies and dismal Desmonds who keep droning on about the dangers of plutonium leaking out from Windscale and bringing an end to civilisation as we know it."

"I say this," Lord Rothschild concluded:

"Bees can be killers. But there are no demonstrations in the streets against the appalling dangers of uncontrolled apiarism."

Lord Rothschild is 81.

Dear Sir,

Our attention has been drawn to the following references in the above article:

1. "absurd peer".

2. "uncontrolled apiarism".

There can be no doubt whatever that these unsubstantiated attacks represent a clear reference to our client Lord Goodchild, Grand Master of Oxford University Challenge. You may rest assured that our client will shortly be issuing rats in a bid for world-domination by means of unleashing teams of highly trained rodents (cont. 1994)

Exclusive

I FIND KAGAN

by Stuart Stephen, Lladislas Farrago and Simone Wiesenthal

After a lifelong search I tracked one of the world's most notorious peace fugitives of post-war years to a hideout in Tel-Aviv today.

He is Herr Martin Kagan — infamous Right-Hand Man to Adolf Wizlon, the self-styled British Fuhrer.

JUST FANCY VAT

For years, officials of Intervat had searched relentlessly for Kagan in all five continents.

Today I can reveal that the master-mind of the infamous Gannex experiments in Barkisland is living under the pseudonym of George Weidenfeld in an exclusive and leafy suburb in the shadow of the Gaza Stilton.

FLYLESS IN GAZA

Neighbours were amazed to learn that this quietly spoken bespectacled sex maniac was the same man who had inflicted indescribable suffering on 89 million mackintosh purchasers.

To them he was simply the kindly old Herr Weidenfeld, known for his love of barbecued Kentucky-style matzoh-balls and his elegant tangos with Rebecca Cadillac, his 17-year-old male nurse.

"I shall be coming home in my own good time," said the fugitive peace-monger today, "or never, whichever is the longer."

Eric Miller is dead.

KEVIN WOODCOCK

SOUTH BARG SHOW
The BENNETT INTERVIEW

(Jazz version of Sanctus from Barg's Mass In B-Minor, arranged for Rees-Mogg Synthesizer by Carlo-Maria von Lloyd-Weber.)

BARG *(for it is he):* One of the most important events in the history of British drama was the recent two-hour television play *Old Rope* by the very talented and distinguished author Alan Bennett. Before we speak to the author, let's just look back at one of the more controversial scenes in his already almost legendary masterpiece.

(Scene shows various actors sitting around table in evening dress.)

1st ACTOR: M-m-m-m. These after-dinner mints are certainly something different.

1st ACTRESS: M-m-m-m. Soft, creamy centres. A hint of Eastern promise, coated in rich, dairy milk chocolate. But then of course Lavinia always had perfect taste.

(Cut to Butler crawling around under table. He smears silk-stockinged leg of lady guest with milk chocolate. Ceiling falls in.)

BARG: Alan, many critics have seen in your play a searing indictment of out-worn middle-class values.

BENNETT: 'appen, life's a challenge, sweetie. I've been deeply shocked by the fact that a lot of illiterate, philistine half-wits living in Tunbridge Wells have failed to recognise me as the exciting and important talent that I am today — with no thanks to my daft Mum.

BARG: That brings me to another masterpiece from this wonderful series of plays which only you and you alone could have written. I am referring to *Early Closing*, the one in which you show a small-town Yorkshire librarian coming to terms with the fact that he is a homosexualist (©J. Betjeman) in a Cleethorpes boarding-house. Shall we just look at a clip of that?

BENNETT: I'd like to see it all — it's so good. I think it's very exciting and important and utterly beguiling (©R. Harty).

(Scene shows bespectacled man in macintosh standing at bus-stop. Young man in T-shirt and tight jeans walks past.)

MAN IN MAC *(shyly):* Excuse me, do you know what time t'bus is due?

BOY IN T-SHIRT: Hullo, Sailor.

(They disappear into nearby cottage. Rain falls.)

EAMONN ANDREWS *(for it is he):* Well, isn't that Alan Bennett all over?

(Hysterical applause from audience.)

ANDREWS: Next week my guests will be Peter Cook, Lord George-Brown and Lulu. See you then.

ENDS

"Happens to them all eventually"

ANOTHER EYE FIRST !

You've seen her on TV! You've read about her in every newspaper in the land! But now, starting this week, Mister Pizza, the Chiswick Batter Mountain, answers your queries about personal problems of all kinds and explains why all men are shits.

Auntie Erin's **Problem Page**

Dear Erin,

My husband gives me £500 a week, and is very loving and caring. What is wrong with my marriage?
CONFUSED, Willesden.

Auntie Erin writes:

You are living in a dream-world. Real life is not like that, as I will testify. Your husband obviously thinks that money can buy everything. Next time he tries to bribe you in this condescending way, you should throw the money back in his face or, better still, send it to me.

Dear Erin,

Every Friday night my husband comes home drunk, and kicks me around the room with his hobnailed boots. I enjoy every minute of it, and frankly this is the only bright spot in my week. Is there something the matter with me, or should I see the doctor?
"BATTERED-AND-LOVING-IT", Tunbridge Wells.

Auntie Erin writes:

Dear Miss Rantzen. You are deluding yourself. You are simply being used as a play-thing. It is high time you settled down and got divorced, like any other healthy girl of your age.

Dear Erin,

My boyfriend and I have been going steady for three years and I am still a virgin. Now our local vicar, who is gay, refuses to marry us. Where have we gone wrong?
KAREN, Islington.

Auntie Erin writes:

I have never received such a disgusting letter in my life. Who do you think you're kidding? No one, that's who. Your vicar is quite right.

Dear Erin,

My hubby and I have been married for five years. We desperately want a love-child, just like everyone else, but my doctor tells me it is impossible so long as we remain married. Is there anything left for people like us to live for?

Auntie Erin says:

This is a cry for help. More and more women in your position are adopting the test-tube love-baby technique, pioneered by Dr Eugene Moneybags. In this way, you may never know who the father of your child is, which is the way it should be if he is to grow up a normal, healthy, maladjusted soccer vandal.

Dear Erin,

I was brought up in a convent school, and was brainwashed for many years into thinking that a woman's role is to be kind and helpful. What can I do about it?
Yours,
BERNADETTE, Liverpool.

Auntie Erin says:

This is the worst evil facing society today. You will have to develop the courage to turn your back on others, and look after Number One. With any luck you will grow up to be a lesbian and then you can appear on BBC religious programmes.

Dear Erin,

I am a black lesbian trapped in a marriage situation with another woman. The worst of it is that I have no one to blame, because there are no men around. Can you advise?
Yours,
ENOLA GAY, Forest Hill.

Auntie Erin says:

This is one of the most difficult problems I have ever had to face. I should blame it all on your father, who sounds to me like the nigger in the woodpile.

Dear Erin,

I am sorry to bother you again *(see above)* but I did not have a father, owing to the fact that I am a love-child.

Continued p. 94

Delfont fails in royal holocaust bid

by **Alessandro Chancellore**,
London Correspondent of *Il Fascisto di Roma*

Looking radiant, and waving her handbag at waiting crowds, the Queen Mother tonight emerged smiling and unscathed from her box at the London Palladium, after an unprecedented eight-hour bombardment of British "entertainment".

The Battling Granny told reporters, "They gave us everything they had — but don't forget my hubby and I lived through the Blitz, and whatever Mr Delfont dishes out, I can take it."

WHO'S THIS GEEZER DELFONT?

For eight hours, the Queen Mum and her entourage were subjected to a non-stop barrage of ancient jokes, numbing dance routines, ageing transvestites, tuneless pop "melodies", singing dogs, men in kilts singing "Och we braw tae Glasgae", and the Don Coggan Steel Band.

She even survived Delfont's new secret weapon, the Doodle-Bygraves, which shut off its engines some years ago and fell last night with an enormous thud in Trafalgar Square.

As the sirens wailed the "All Clear", the Queen Mother stepped forward through the rubble and broken glass to shake hands with her arch-enemy, Lord Delfont.

"Let Bygraves be Bygraves," she said with a radiant smile.

Lord Delfont is 104.

STRIKE HALTS WORLD WAR THREE

by Our Defence Staff
C.N.D. MARCH

An unofficial strike by members of Mr Moss Evans's 8-million strong Transport Workers Union today brought a temporary halt to the Royal Navy's attempt to counter a 'pre-emptive nuclear strike' by Warsaw Pact countries against the West.

Shortly after NATO radar screens revealed that Soviet missiles were heading for targets in Britain, cleaners at the top-secret Rosyth Naval Base 'downed tools'.

The result of this unofficial action, according to a spokesman, was that "Britain was unable to provide an appropriate response to the nuclear war situation."

It is understood that well over 40 million Britons died in the resulting holocaust.

A spokesman for the TGWU said later: "We deeply regret any inconvenience to the public that may have been caused by our action, but it is time that management realised that our members are carrying out a highly responsible job, with the lives of millions at stake, and frankly, 500 quid a week is not much to ask for."

Let's face it, letter-writing is a thing of the past. Something out of the age of the horse-and-cart.

All right for Grandad, maybe. But, quite honestly, in the world of the tele-communications satellite, your fuddy-duddy old letter makes you look a real old-fashioned square.

Get with it! Put away your quill pen and tune in to the twentieth century.

Get knotted.

Someone somewhere may be wanting a letter from you

But remember — there may be a few little problems!

For example — you may find it difficult to buy a stamp.

Your friendly neighbourhood pillar box may have a metal plate over the opening, labelled "CLOSED UNTIL FURTHER NOTICE".

Even if you do find a stamp and a pillar box, you could still be in trouble.

For instance, your letter might not be cleared for several days. It might become one of the 75 million letters-too-many which are cluttering up Britain's sorting offices.

In fact, you'll be lucky if your letter ever gets sorted at all — let alone delivered.

BE SENSIBLE. Why waste your time and ours writing letters in the first place?

A Doctor writes

John Cleese

I am often told by worried patients, "Doctor, I don't laugh at John Cleese — is there anything wrong?"

Well, the short answer is no. John Cleese, or *Borus Basilius Manicus* as he is known to the medical profession, is a tall moustachioed person who appears on television from time to time.

Research shows that quite a number of people — just how many we doctors do not at the moment know — show the following symptoms: their facial expressions register bewilderment and frustration, and in some cases irritation of a mild variety.

If you yourself do not laugh at John Cleese, there is nothing whatever to worry about. But if you are in any doubt you should seek psychiatric help.

©*'A Doctor'. 1979*

It's Your Line to
GEORGE G.ALE

MAN: Hullo George, first-time caller from Catford. Nice to speak to you.

ALE: Yes, yes, get on with it.

MAN: My point is this, George. Everywhere you look today you see this 'Talbot!' written up. Take my street, for instance, which is called Talbot Road, incidentally.

ALE: Really?

MAN: Yes, well, that's not the point, though. What I mean is, what is this 'Talbot' thing they're all talking about? I mean, I'm a cab-driver. I'm self-employed. I'm not a Conservative, although I've got nothing against Mrs Thatcher. But everywhere you look, it's Talbot this and Talbot that. I mean, they've even brought out this magazine called *Talbot!*, which frankly to my mind is a lot of rubbish. They leave 'em in my cab, George, hundreds of 'em. Anyway, George, what I'd just like to know is this. . .

ALE: Yes, what's that?

MAN: Is this Talbot a man, or what?

ALE: Thank you, and now we'll go to Paul Johnson from Sydenham. . .

New 'Pakenham' discovered

By Our Salesroom Corres- pondent *Geraldine Back-to- normal-in-six-months'-time- if-you're-lucky*

A team of literary ex- perts headed by the legendary Dr Michael Wharton have made what promises to be one of the most exciting new 'literary finds' for years.

Dr Wharton has unearthed a hitherto completely unknown member of the celebrated 'Longford writing dynasty', in the shape of Lady Doreen Nargs (formerly Pakenham).

Lady Doreen is a younger sister of the more famous Lady Magnesia Freelove, and also Dr Kevin Pakenham, whose monumental history of the war between El Salvador and Nicaragua in 1821 is shortly to be published by Snipcock and Tweed.

Among other members of the celebrated family are, of course, Lord Longford him- self, Lady Longjohns, author of the recent widely-acclaimed biography of Lord "Nancy" Cunargs, Lady Rachel Heyhoe- Billingsgate, Lady Unity Mitbarg and a cast of thousands.

Same Old Targets

Lady Doreen, who lives in a disused coal barge in Fulham with her unemployed working- class *Time Out* film critic husband "Josh" Nargs, has written 123 novels, all of which are to be published next month in a special "Collectors' Edition" by Snipcock and Tweed.

She was also the author of last night's controversial BBC2 "Play For Yesterday", *Come Off It*, which explored the problem of battered love- parents in single-child family situations.

A Woman's Right to Cheese

From Ms Jill Tweedie and others.

Dear Sir,

We represent millions of women in all walks of life. We have read with growing con- cern the above item, with its blatantly sexist overtones and total disregard for the plight of the billions of women who are being battered to death against their will at this very moment in time. There are legitimate targets for satire — e.g. Mrs Thatcher, Mrs White- house, Barbara Cartland — but women are not one of them. Since time began, women have been singled out for oppression. The earliest cave paintings show pictures of enormous women being trampled to death by dinosaurs. It is time this sort of thing stopped.

Sisterly greetings,

JILL TWEEDIE, IRMA KURSE, ANNA RAEBURN- YOURBRA, ERIN BATTERMOUNTAIN, CLAIRE RAINOR- SHEIN et al (believed to be a reference to the late Alan Brien who was forced to sign this letter at gunpoint).

Letter

From Sir Herbert Gussett

SIR—I was interested to read in your columns the account of the vicar who shot a sparrow that had interrupted a punk-rock concert in his church.

Those of us who have experience of such matters will cry as one "Hats off!" Many years ago it was my privilege to attend a xylophone recital given by my friend Lt. Col. "Buffy" Frobisher at the Church of St Rumpole in the little Dorset village of Wyfe-Battering. A large audience in the shape of my lady wife and I had gathered in the nave to hear the Colonel give his rendering of the Horst Wessel Song (arr. for xylophone by B. Frobisher). It is perhaps relevant to note that the year was 1939.

The few of us privileged to be familiar with the title know only too well the artistic strains placed upon the performer and the compelling need for complete silence in the auditorium. We settled in our pews, and an expectant hush fell on the tiny church. Imagine the dismay when a giant thrush swooped down from the belfry, emitting a characteristic mating call and flapping its enormous wings above our heads.

Luckily for all and sundry I had had the foresight to bring with me my trusty shotgun and some aerosol cans of poison gas. So it was that within seconds the huge bird lay lifeless at our feet, its multi-coloured wings flapping in their last final frenzy.

Needless to say, there was at that time no shortage of critics of my decisive action. Of course, Sir, as I pointed out, we have a duty to our feathered friends, as indeed we have to the myriad scaly creatures who accompany us along life's dusty path. My reply then remains valid today. The thrush in question had uttered its seductive call. Had it been allowed to live, within seconds the church would have been invaded by a feathered throng of panting females too hideous to contemplate. Furthermore it is inconceivable that the recital could have continued if Buffy's artistry had been subjected to the unearthly warblings of this giant bird.

There was only one unfortunate repercussion. The incumbent of St Rumpole's was struck by a hail of ricocheting pellets, and fell to the floor as if dead. Subsequent investigation by Dr Gleadle and his skilled team of surgeons showed this indeed to be the case.

On the other hand, what better way to go than to be killed instantaneously whilst suffused with pleasurable anticipation of a recital that will live on in my memory for centuries?

When my time comes, as indeed it must, I fervently pray that I shall be blown off a cliff by a freak gust of wind while Buffy plays a selection of Lita Roza's biggest hits on his harmonica.

I remain, Sir,

HERBERT GUSSETT
Delirium St Tremens
Hornby, Lincs

Observer Village Guide

(continued from p. 94)

Gussett Parva

Fairly unattractive, mostly modern village. One house on council estate has roses around the door. Birthplace of Alan Coren. Interesting Victorian font in church. Real Ale available at local Spart supermarket.

Winterbourne Gussett

Interesting old manor house has been converted to corn-dolly craft workshop, run by ex-publisher. Interesting old ironwork in village pond. Local garage sells Real Ale.

Lower Frobisher

Wonderful views of the Mould. Hand-woven duvets on sale at Wessex Traditional Duvet Centre in converted Methodist chapel. Real Ale available from local sewage farm.

Activities

Walking (no permits required)

Information Centres

Frobisher Episcopi, Wheatcroft-on-the-Floor

Houses open to the public

Pottinger Manor: unusual dovecote. Garden centre.
Badger Hall: bicycle museum and Victorian kitchen sinks.

Where to stay

The Socialist Guest House, 'Dunprotestin', 137 Station Road, Longford-on-Make. Mr & Mrs Roger Protz serve Real Ale for breakfast. Brown rice under pictures of Trotsky, Guevara etc. Comrades only.

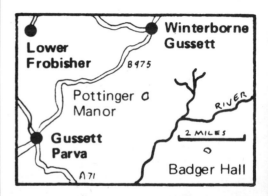

"When I was a boy we had to make our own entertainment"

"It's a digital sun-dial, dear"

Gussett of The Antarctic

Recluse sues

by Our Polar Correspondent
Norman St. John-Brumas

A new book which claims to shed light on the ill-fated Gussett Polar Expedition of 1923 may never now see the light of day, following a writ served on the publishers yesterday by the explorer's great-nephew, Sir Herbert Gussett, the Dorset naturalist and antiquarian.

The book, by journalist Kevin Protz, alleges that Captain Ferdinand Wilberforce Gussett, so-called "Conqueror of the Poles", never in fact got any nearer to the Arctic regions than Fulham.

SHOCK

The world waited agog in 1923 for the outcome of the much-publicised "Race to the Pole" between the team led by Captain Gussett and a scratch crew of Lithuanians sponsored by the German fish-paste king, Sir Jams Himmler.

At first Himmler seemed to race ahead, with his mechanised dogs and hydrofoil sleighs. Capt. Gussett refused point-blank to travel to the Pole by any other means than on his hands and knees.

By 1927 it was clear that the German/Lithuanian team had won.

But it is only recently that hitherto unpublished letters have revealed the real reason why Sir Jams won the day.

In fact Capt. Gussett never set off at all, and spent the year in question "holed up in the Snug Bar of the Wheatcroft Arms, Dollis Road, Fulham."

AMAZING

Sir Herbert said yesterday, "I have not read Mr Protz's book, but it is clearly a vile slur on the name of a very gallant English gentleman.

"I had allowed Mr Protz access to my scrapbooks and memorabilia (slightly foxed) on the strict understanding that he would not read them.

"Now this confidence has been shamelessly abused, and the cat is out of the bag."

Sir Herbert is 107.

BLOW YOUR OWN NOSE 10p

·MADDOCKS·

Toadthrush in bed~fall drama

New blow to beleagured President

from Our Man in Washington
SIR PETER JAY-TALBOT

As his popularity slumped to a new all-time low, President Toadthrush was yesterday involved in yet another incident of the type that has rocked the White House during his incumbency.

It was revealed today that the President had last night "fallen out of bed" while still asleep.

Amazing

Medical experts were quick to point out that there was nothing unusual in a man of the President's age falling out of bed for no apparent reason.

Nevertheless, the fall is being widely interpreted here as yet another sign of the President's failing powers.

As a disillusioned White House Staffer put it to me today: "Soon this guy won't even be able to put his butt on the can."

Turd Flush

While preparing for tonight's nationwide TV speech, in which he had hoped to minimise his "bed fall incident" by drawing attention to the CIA's recent discovery of Soviet combat troops in the Oval Office of the White House, President Toadthrush this afternoon fell heavily while he was "in the bathroom".

Aides later explained that the President had been attacked by a "killer ladybird" while "meditating" on tonight's keynote speech.

President's mother in new storm

A new row today erupted in the Democratic Party following controversial remarks made by the President's mother, Ms Lilian Hellman, during a fundraising "Kentucky bar'b'que" at New Talbot, Mass.

Ms Hellman, 106, told 3,000 bewildered party workers: "I heah that Teddy is thinkin' of runnin' against mah boy.

"I sho' hope some goddam gunman doesn't get any fancy notions of blastin' his brains out, like those po' dead brothers of his (lawdy, lawdy!).

"Mind you, you'd sho' have to be a crack shot to discover any brains in Teddy's head!

"I don't mean no disrespect. I'm sho' Teddy's a perfectly nice boy — the kind you could trust to run your daughter home after a party, without knowin' she'll end up at the bottom of the ocean.

"And I sho' hope the spirit of po' little Mary-Jo don't come back and haunt him nights. Why, shucks, even a blind hog can find an acre to pee in sometimes."

Later, in a White House clarification, a press aide said: "The President's mother was widely misreported, owing to her unfamiliar Southern accent.

"She has the greatest respect for Senator Kennedy, and wishes him nothing but success in overcoming his drug problem."

Lunch of lunches

LADY ELIZABETH LONGJOHNS

MAKE NO MISTAKE — all of literary London will be there at Burp's Restaurant, Charlotte Street, for the publishing event of the year on 27 July — the already-world-famous Gnome Literary Luncheon.

This year's guest of honour will be the celebrated historian and biographer, Lady Elizabeth Longjohns, whose latest book is certain to become one of the most talked-about bits of rubbish ever published by Snipcock and Tweed.

Lady Longjohns' latest subject is the celebrated Edwardian explorer, poet and homosexualist, Sir Wilfred Hyde-Gussett.

Rubbish

Sir Wilfred knew all the most famous figures of his day — Lord Henry Nargs, Lady Margot Thing, and "Skittles", the celebrated *poule-de-luxe*, whose elegant Mayfair soirees were regularly attended by some of the most famous figures of the day, including Lord Henry Nargs and Lady Margot Thing.

But the real bombshell in Lady Longjohns' brilliantly researched biography is her disclosure, with the help of hitherto secret diaries, that all his life Lord Wilfred did absolutely nothing of any interest whatsoever.

Jawn Wells

Among the glittering literati who will be free-loading at the Gnome Lunch will be Mr Melvyn Barg, the Lakeland Poet, Mr Ronald Bargwood, "TV's Man of Letters", Lady Magnesia Free-loader and her friend Mr Harold Wintour, Sir Charles Mostyn-Pintour and his friend, Lady Flame-Haired Temptress, Mr Peter Forster and Mr Allan Hall, Wine and Food Correspondent of the magazine *New!*

YOU TOO can mingle with the mighty at the Lord Gnome Literary Lunch.

A few thousand tickets, costing £28 each, are still available from Gnome Literary Promotions Ltd, c/o *Evening Standard*, Shoe Lane, EC4.

Masonic News

MR R.B.J. Supergrass, Chief Grand Prior and Provisional Supervisor of the Provincial Grand Order of Wardrobes and Dr N.C.Q. Homosexualist, Deputy Grand Almoner In Ordinary to the Supreme Vice Master of Lodges, presided at the annual Ceremony of Tables (Nuneaton).

Guests included Dr M.M.C. Boxwallah-Boxwallah, Grand Commander of the Temple (Bletchley), Rev. C.P.G. Marx-Brothers, Chaplain In Ordinary to the Chief Grand Supreme Rubbish (Tunbridge Wells) and S.S.V. Gummidge (Hartley Wintney).

Mr R.D. Self-Abuse was ordained as Lower Marshal to the Knights of the Inner Chapter (Carshalton).

"For God's sake, Richard, it's only an owl! — You've got Wedgwood Benn on the brain!"

"Join me on the voyage of discovery to your inner self"

says world-famous columnist **BERNARD LEVIN**

Ever since the dawn of time itself, man has sought to unravel the secrets of the universe. Now, thanks to a wonderful new discovery made in America, I can offer you a chance to share in the most exciting journey you will ever make — the voyage into the VERY DEPTHS OF YOUR OWN BEING!

For only £500 (+ VAT) you too can have three days, absolutely free, at the Institute For Inner Awareness.

Let famous TV personality Arianna Stassinopoulos be your guide on this mission into the unknown continent that is the 'inner you'.

After just three days 'on the path', we guarantee that you will have

> LESS aggression
> LESS hang-ups
> LESS money

and that you will enjoy

> MORE caring
> MORE sharing
> MORE inner fulfilment in the marriage situation.

For more details, just send s.a.e. (plus £300 signing-on fee) to:

> **INNER VACATIONS** c/o Holiday Inn, London Airport.

Famous Editor W.R.M. writes

"For years, the cares of running a famous newspaper were like a large cathedral round my neck. I was in a permanent stress situation. But, since my friend Mr Levin introduced me to the Inner Way of Happiness, my life has been transformed. I stay at home all day and experience true inner bliss."

U.S. Affairs

MANSON THROWS HAT IN RING

by Our Washington Staff
HENRY FAIRLIE-BORING

The US political scene was rocked to its foundations yesterday when 'sixties cult figure Charles Manson threw down the gauntlet in a direct personal challenge to President Toadthrush for next year's Democratic nomination.

For months now there has been growing pressure on Manson to declare himself as a candidate, despite the admitted 'lapses of judgement' back in 1969 which had seemed to cast doubt on his credibility as would-be leader of the free world.

Better Dead Than Ted

But in recent years there has been a growing popular desire in America for the return of a truly charismatic leader in the White House.

And one thing that is certain is that Manson arouses unswerving loyalty in his followers.

Averred a worried Toadthrush staffer: "Sure this guy was into homicide — but these days the man in the street is more worried by inflation and the energy crisis than he is by some poor crazy girl getting bumped off back in the 'sixties."

In a revealing interview on nationwide television, Senator Manson recently went over in detail the alleged events of 1969.

"If I erred on that occasion," said the new Presidential hopeful, "that is something I have to live with every day of my life. But what may or may not have happened is irrelevant to the needs of a country searching for its identity.

"But I say this. If I had to do it all over again to save America from another four years of drift and uncertainty I would have no hesitation."

Senator Manson was given a standing ovation by an audience of fellow prisoners at New Talbot Penitentiary, San Clemente, California.

"Just because I've got an ice-pick in my head doesn't mean I'm a Trotskyist!"

After Th

By
Sylvie Krin

the spell-binding novelist who brought

you *LOVE IN THE SADDLE, AMOROSO*

and *RODDY IS MY DARLING.*

The story so far:

Anna Ford, a simple country girl in her early twenties, has come to London for the January sales.

To her surprise, she is chosen from hundreds of women to become ITN's answer to Angela Rippon.

At the studio she meets for the first time, bluff, convivial, hard-living Ronnie Beaujolais.

NOW READ ON:

The clock on the studio wall showed two minutes to ten. The dapper figure of Kevin Meaker, the studio manager, called: "Quiet, studio. We go in two."

It was the night of Anna's debut as a fully-fledged newscasterette. The eyes of the world would be on her. And she could be sure that her arch-rival, the glacial Angela Rippon, would be sharpening her claws in anticipation of the slightest slip.

Outwardly, Anna was calm. But inside there was turmoil. Two minutes, she said to herself. And still the chair at her side was empty. Where was he?

Her eyes sent a silent plea to Meaker, who sat imperviously, rubbing a spot of grease from his tight-fitting suede trousers.

Where was he. . . ?

"Start the clock. One minute."

Anna began to rifle through the papers. Supposing he didn't arrive, what then? Would she have to dart from chair to chair?

As the seconds ticked away on the big studio clock, her mind raced back over the events of the day — a day which had promised so much, but which now seemed destined to end in disaster.

The morning had begun so brightly. The press conference full of cheery newsmen, asking probing but always friendly questions.

"Favourite colour?"

"Blue."

That had gone down well.

And all the time at her side, the friendly, almost paternal, presence of her lifetime idol, Ronnie Beaujolais. From the start he had taken her under his wing, introducing her to that elite club of TV personalities who were household names up and down the country.

Randy Gaul, the veteran South African war reporter with his risque golfing stories. Alistair Brunette, the ruthless political mastermind. Colourful West Indian Trevor Barbados, famous for his spontaneous limbo dancing at Fund-Raising Dinners.

And now she was one of them.

"Thirty seconds!"

And still the chair at her side was empty. The clock ticked inexorably on. Five! Four! Three! Two! One!

The music swelled in its familiar ominous tones. The great bell of Big Ben tolled out.

Boing!

Still no Ronnie.

Boing!

There was a crash behind her, the sound of distant laughter and breaking glass, and before she knew what was happening television's most charismatic male was at her side.

She felt a reassuring hand on her thigh and a strange aroma assaulted her pert nostrils.

Not in a million years had she dreamed it would be like this.

CHAPTER II

No one seemed surprised by Ronnie's last-minute arrival in the studio. Just as Big Ben began to chime, the rubicund broadcaster had crashed through the screen behind her and slumped into his chair.

And yet the studio manager Kevin Meaker had scarcely raised an eyebrow. To him it was plainly a nightly ritual.

As Ronnie began to read the headlines, Anna's heart skipped a beat. How would it end? Perhaps she would have to take over. She steeled herself for this eventuality.

But her fears were unfounded. As if transformed, Ronnie stared straight into the camera and announced with a clear voice:

"Ambulance Men. Callaghan spells it out.

"Sewage workers go back.

"But grave diggers stand firm."

It was amazing. A moment ago Ronnie had been crawling on the floor like a drowning man. But now he was as millions of viewers knew him, with all the poise of an old pro.

Soon he had completed his round-up and it was her turn. Kevin Meaker "cued her in".

She heard herself saying, "Snow ploughs were out at dawn today as millions of motorists began the long crawl home." But her thoughts were not on what she was reading.

Something was wrong. She could hear a strange noise of liquid pouring into a glass, and from the corner of her eye she glimpsed Ronnie Beaujolais emptying the contents of a green medicine bottle into a tumbler.

Furtively, he gulped down the amber fluid and a warm smile spread over his

ruddy features.

Anna tried to concentrate on her lines. Gripping her sheaf of notes, she read:

"And Britain's Met Men say There's More To Come."

That was the item she had dreaded.

Now Ronnie took over again. If possible there was even more confidence in his voice and his lips shone brightly in the harsh studio lights. Anna marvelled at his aplomb as his gravelly voice caressed each word.

"In Part Two. The Lighthouse with too much Grit. The Car that runs on marmalade. And why Horace the Hippo is looking for a Kidney Donor. Join us again."

At last the break had come. The first part of her ordeal was over. Relieved, she looked across at Ronnie for reassurance.

But he was pouring out another glass of medicine — this time a colourless fluid from a thermos flask.

"Are you alright?" she asked him in trepidation. He didn't hear. All his concentration seemed focussed on the delicate act of pouring.

"Is there anything I can do?" she persevered.

Then he looked up and for the first time seemed aware of her presence and her anxious gaze.

He tapped the thermos.

"Medicine," he said. "Doctor's orders. War Wound. Korea. '52. Sharp End. Don't like to talk about it. Less said the better."

So that was it.

Poor Ronnie. Behind the jovial mask, behind the man who nightly intoned the sufferings of others, lay an invalid wracked by pain — a war hero too modest to tell the world of his courage.

A voice inside told her that a schoolgirl's crush was burgeoning into a deeper emotion. Something she feared — and at the same time found irresistible.

CHAPTER III

"In Part Two — Corpses: The Chancellor Counts The Cost. New Hope For Denture Wearers. And the Mynah Bird that failed the Virgin Test. Join Us Again."

Anna still marvelled at the cool efficiency with which Ronnie brought the end of Part One of *News At Ten* to a fitting climax.

No wonder millions of viewers were glued to their sets.

Now it was time for his medicine. After three weeks Anna was familiar with this nightly ritual and each time her yearning heart opened out to the war veteran suffering in silence at her side.

She wanted desperately to tell him of her feelings towards him. But three minutes was not long enough. How could one speak of things so intimate while hundreds of technicians sat idly around, playing cards and counting their wage packets?

And could she trust the Studio Manager, Kevin Meaker? There was something sinister about him. After her very first newscast he had sidled up to her and whispered savagely in her ear, "Lay off Ronnie, sweetie. He's mine."

What could he mean?

*   *   *

The hospitality room at ITN was crowded as usual. It was like a club. As Anna entered the room her eyes scanned the familiar figures — Randy Gaul, looking sun-tanned from his trip to war-torn Seychelles; Trevor Barbados, famous for his spontaneous limbo-dancing at fund-raising dinners; Alistair Brunette, as suave as ever, his pink gin perfectly matching the neatly folded copy of the *Financial Times* under his arm.

And at the centre of the group — Ronnie. Laughing, singing, juggling with beer-bottle tops. What a brave facade, she thought.

Her heart missed a beat. For as soon as he saw her Ronnie detached himself from the group and, with his hands outstretched, staggered towards her.

"Hullo, Miss Ford," he drawled. "What's your poison?"

The blood rushed to her cheeks and before she knew what was happening she found herself seated alone with Ronnie in a corner of the bar.

She was unfamiliar with the cocktail he had selected — a Mexican Bollock-Shaker, he had called it, telling her that it had to be swallowed in one gulp to avoid giving offence to the natives.

Now she lifted the glass to her full lips and suddenly became aware of the silence.

All eyes were on her. It was plainly another initiation ceremony of some kind, but one which for Ronnie's sake she would gladly undergo.

She steeled herself and poured the bright green fluid down her delicately fashioned throat.

Anna had never experienced anything like it before. Multi-coloured stars exploded before her eyes. Bongo drums pounded savagely within her bosom. The rancid overpowering aroma of the Mexican rain forests was all about her.

Was this love? The feeling expressed by a million poets down the ages?

The room went dark. And the last thing she could remember was the sound of hollow, raucous laughter.

CHAPTER IV

I t was Anna's first night off for months. She had been News-at-Tenning for as long, it seemed, as she could remember.

And now she sat among the guests of honour at the Foyles International Year of the Woman Dinner at the Dorchester Hotel.

While waiters moved obsequiously among the seated guests, Anna surveyed the dazzling scene with an excitement she could scarcely conceal.

Little had she dreamed in her carefree childhood years that one day she would sit in the company of such illustrious names as Edna O'Brien and Jean Rook.

Across the room she espied the reassuring figure of Barbara Cartland. And wasn't that Esther Rantzen breast-feeding her child, watched by the admiring figure of Maureen Colquhoun MP?

Now the coffee was served and as the clatter of cutlery died away the toast-person rose to her feet to announce: "My ladies, pray silence for tonight's Guest of Honour — Ms Angela Rippon."

A storm of applause broke on the air as the slim, perfectly coiffed *doyenne* of the newsroom rose to her feet like a graceful heron.

A strange sensation passed through Anna's perfectly formed body. For was not this her supposed rival? Were they not, if the papers were to be believed, locked in deadly combat for the eyes of the nation?

But as Angela began to speak in her familiar icy tones, Anna could feel only admiration mingled with awe. She listened enraptured as the carefully modulated speech pierced the ever-thickening clouds of cigar smoke.

"Women are no longer chained," she was saying. "Gone are the days when

young girls could be swept off their feet by ageing Lotharios and ruthless Romeos. Our message goes out, clear and shrill. The woman of today is her own mistress."

Tumultuous applause greeted this ringing declaration. The assembled ladies rose as a man, and Anna found herself suddenly standing next to her rival. She was shaking her hand and saying, "Angela! Angela! You don't know me. But I am Anna Ford. I just want to say how marvellous you are and how I do so agree with all that you say."

Angela smiled winningly. "My dear, of course I know who you are. The best of luck to you in your new job. And don't forget. We women must steer well clear of those men."

And before Anna could reply, Angela was swept off by a crowd of admirers.

Anna looked at her watch. 10.15! It was time to go. She joined the phalanx of Britain's leading women as they queued for their furs and track-suits.

The heady excitement was wearing off and suddenly Anna felt very much alone. It was then that out of the corner of her eye she saw him, on the screen in the corner of the Hotel's lavish foyer.

Her heart leapt and, forgetting her coat, she ran towards the set, brushing aside the hordes of waiting Arabs.

"In Part Two. The jogger who married his mother. British Leyland — the Government says "Why?" And will Horace the Cuckoo get a 10% rise? Join us again in a couple of minutes."

Anna was overwhelmed by a tide of emotions. She heard herself saying, "Oh Ronnie, Ronnie! I will join you again any time, any place, anywhere. You're the right one, you're the bright one, you're my Ronnie!"

A voice shattered her reverie.

"I think this is your coat, Miss Ford."

She turned abruptly to find the steely eyes of Angela Rippon boring into her own. She said nothing, but Angela's hawk-like gaze told Anna that she had been found wanting.

Grabbing her coat, she ran sobbing out into the night.

CHAPTER V

It was Easter-time. Anna looked out over the sundrenched Cumbrian moorland, now ablaze with daffodils, from the perfectly formed window of her bedroom.

Her eyes feasted on the familiar scenes of childhood. It was here that as a little girl she had run barefoot on the moss-covered hills, communing with nature, while her father, Dr Ford, a veterinary surgeon of some 60 years, treated an endless parade of sick animals in his surgery below.

From tired old carthorses to tiny hamsters, the dedicated silver-haired vet and part-time lay preacher had cared for all of them.

It was good to be back. *News At Ten* had not been easy, with the hurly-burly of election fever. And meanwhile Ronnie had seemed almost oblivious of her.

She was therefore all the more surprised when he accepted her invitation to spend a two-day break here at her family home.

One thing was certain, she assured him. The fresh air and her mother's home cooking would soon do wonders to restore his health and confidence.

The spare room was ready for him. She herself had spent all morning making it spick and span with her own perfectly formed hands. She had picked a posy of violets and bluebells to place beside the bottle of Lucozade on the bedside table.

★　　★　　★

The grandfather clock chimed a quarter past ten. Suppertime at the Fords' was a simple affair. They sat, their "telly-snacks" delicately balanced on their knees, watching the flickering black and white screen on the sideboard.

The suave, aristocratic features of Sir

Julian de Brabazon, ITN's chief political correspondent, looked blurred and ghost-like as he proclaimed:

"In Part Two. Mr Pardoe spells it out to Britain's greengrocers. Why the islanders of Tobago want to be paid in coconuts. And why Wally the Lamb wouldn't eat his Hot Cross Bun. Join us again in a couple of minutes."

Mrs Ford looked up from her knitting. "Tell me, Anna, what's he like, this Ronnie friend of yours who's coming to stay? Your father and I often have difficulty in understanding what he's saying, don't we dear?"

Dr Jolyon sipped thoughtfully at his home-made elderberry whisky. "It's the set, if you ask me, Daphne," he replied as he refilled his pipe. "I've been onto Braggs a million times to come and fix it.

Anyway, what's it matter? It's all a lot of nonsense."

Her mother sighed and resumed her crochet-work. The old clock ticked quietly in the corner of the room. For some reason Anna felt a sense of deep foreboding about Ronnie's arrival the following day. How would this suave man-about-town react to their simple country pleasures?

A few minutes later, she arose and, wishing her parents 'Goodnight', went upstairs. As she turned out the light she assured herself that everything would be all right.

★   ★   ★

Anna stood on the platform with her father, waiting for the Keswick train to appear round the bend.

The old man took his gold hunter watch from his thick tweed waistcoat pocket and announced that Ronnie should be there any second.

"I expect he'll find us a bit stick-in-the-mud, this Ronnie of yours," he said, patting her affectionately on her perfectly formed arm. "Still my dear, if you've taken a shine to him your mother and I won't stand in your way."

Before she could reply, a whistle sounded and the Keswick express roared to a standstill beside them.

Suddenly the platform was filled with bustling figures clutching their heavy suit-cases as they greeted friends and loved ones.

Anna's eyes anxiously searched the scurrying throng for a sign of her hero. Her heart beat faster. Where was he? Within a few moments the platform had emptied and the train was drawing away.

Suddenly the door of a rear compartment in the slowly moving train was flung open, and with a cry of "Hold it, you daft beggars!" Ronnie fell onto the platform, clutching his familiar plastic bag.

With screeching brakes the train jolted to a halt as a large dusky lady in red satin hot-pants and thigh-length green suede boots fell on top of him.

Apparently unharmed, the dishevelled figure of the nation's Number One newscaster picked himself up and stumbled towards them.

"Hullo, old girl!" he beamed. "I want you to meet — what's your name, darling? You don't mind if she comes to stay with you for a few days, do you Anna? We met at Euston.

"Apparently she's a fantastic limbo dancer," he added, nudging Dr Ford conspiratorially in the ribs.

Anna felt the tears well up and then they came bursting out, as her perfectly formed body quivered with shame, jealousy and disappointment.

CHAPTER VI

It was pay day. The bar at ITN House was unusually crowded. All "the Boys" were there, waiting for ten o'clock to come. As she entered, Anna could see the familiar group huddled around "their" table.

Alistair Brunette, his pink cheeks flushed with good health. Trevor Barbados, famous for his spontaneous limbo-dancing at fund-raising dinners. Randy Gaul, his world-weary features for once relaxed and smiling.

Suddenly, as Anna approached, the room was filled with a roar of hearty masculine laughter. She noticed a copy of the *Daily Mirror* lying half-sodden on the table, covered with empty glasses.

"Here you are, Anna," cried Gaul, rising unsteadily to his feet. "Want a good laugh? Old Ronnie's been up to his tricks again, by the look of things."

His remark triggered off a renewed burst of laughter as Anna took the newspaper and read the tell-tale headline:

My Naughty Nights With Ronnie: "Love Child" Mother Tells All.

Over the months Anna had been used to reading stories of a sensational and often unpleasant sort.

But these words shocked her petite frame. She felt her perfectly formed stomach go cold as she read the details of a sordid court case in which "her Ronnie", as she now thought of him, had played a central part.

Bluebeard. Svengali. Drink problem. These were the tell-tale phrases that reverberated in her innocent and impressionable mind.

"Give the bugger an inch and he'll take a mile," somebody said. And once again her Dresden ears were assaulted by the crude guffaws of her colleagues.

Suddenly a hush fell on the assembled newscasters and Anna turned to see Him, pushing his way doggedly through the crowded room.

"KV chaps!" cried Trevor Barbados in his impeccable accent. "It's Big Daddy-O!"

Before Anna could speak, Ronnie, his eyes blazing with anger, snatched up the newspaper and, tearing it into shreds, scattered the fragments like confetti in all directions.

"Lies! Lies!" he screamed. "I shall l sue. Writs! Writs!"

And then, suddenly, pathetically, he crumpled, and slumped sobbing onto the bar, his head buried in his hands.

Anna was by his side. She wanted to touch and console him but she knew the others would only mock.

Instead she whispered into his ear words of comfort. Looking up, he said: "You believe me, old girl, don't you? I've done some rum things in my day, but I'd never get a girl into trouble and leave her in the lurch."

*   *   *

"In Part Two. Scottish Nationalists say Yes to Healey's package. Britain's Rose-growers want a better deal. And why Tuffy the Squirrel gave away his nuts. Join us in a couple of minutes."

Ronnie was still in an emotional state, Anna thought, although his ten million fans would never have known. She noticed that his hand trembled as he poured the now-familiar bright green medicine into a plastic beaker.   •

Now more than ever she wanted to say, "Yes Ronnie, I believe you. Of course I do." But before she could speak they were back on the air and she found herself saying:

"Winter returned to may parts of Britain today. On Humberside snow ploughs were out at dawn to try to free stranded motorists."

The film showing the traditional winter scenes began. And it was then that Anna noticed the slip of paper on her script.

A late newsflash item, she thought to herself. She read it quickly, for she was to be back "on camera" in thirty seconds.

Her cheeks flushed uncontrollably as she read the tell-tale message: "You look great tonight, Big Eyes. How about a spot of supper back at my place? Ronnie."

In her perfectly formed mind she seemed to hear the hollow sound of men laughing far away in some distant saloon.

CHAPTER VII

The sound of popping champagne corks could be heard all over ITN House. The party to celebrate Anna's engagement was in full swing. In the main reception room, the furniture had been pushed aside to make room for the dancing revellers.

In one corner all three members of the Chappie d'Amato Big Band pounded out a cha-cha-cha version of the News At Ten theme.

Anna, clutching the arm of her beau, surveyed the scene in an ecstasy of confused emotions.

There was Alistair Brunette, his healthy pink face running with perspiration and Brut as he danced cheek-to-knee with Janet Street Walker.

And across the room, clutching the generous form of Joan Furrykettle from the newsroom, Randy Gaul, his tie askew and his hair dishevelled, was shouting like a banshee as the intoxicating rhythms of the d'Amato Band excited him to further feats of frenzy.

In the centre of the floor a group of guests were clapping ecstatically as Trevor Barbados, stripped to the waist and balancing a bottle of rum on his head, attempted to limbo-dance under a table laden with jellies.

Anna felt a strong arm encircling her waist.

"Gosh," said John Snargs, smiling blissfully into her eyes, "isn't it wonderful? And yet we still have so much to learn about each other."

She nestled up to him and felt momentarily reassured.

It was then that suddenly, out of the corner of her perfectly formed eye, she saw a familiar figure bursting through the swing door at the far end of the room, a bottle of medicine in one hand and that familiar plastic carrier bag in the other.

As he swayed onto the dancefloor like a wounded rhinoceros, the dancing

couples drifted to the sidelines to allow him free passage.

A hush fell over the room.

The band, sensing a change of mood, struck up the *Police Five* Waltz.

Now he was at her side, peering through war-torn eyes at her youthful fiance.

"What's going on?" he yelled, waving his medicine bottle above his head. "Not Christmas yet, is it?"

There were sniggers now from the revellers standing nervously in the wings, sensing that something was amiss. Ronnie had that effect on people.

And now he fixed John Snargs with a steely gaze from his bloodshot eyes. Thinly disguised contempt shone from every pore of his pain-wracked visage.

"Who the bloody hell d'you think you are, laddy?" he snarled.

"Ronnie! Ronnie!" Anna pleaded, her perfectly formed lips trembling with emotion. "This is John! We're engaged to be married!"

"No you're bloody well not!" roared Ronnie, grabbing young Snargs by the collar of his flowered shirt. "You're engaged to be married to one of those ITN pansy-boys! It's all in the paper."

Before she could explain, Ronnie had swung a crudely aimed blow with his clanking carrier bag at the startled Snargs.

But the young roving reporter was too swift for the war veteran's clumsy lunge.

With one crack of his clenched fist he sent Ronnie sprawling across the room towards the jelly-laden table beneath which the lissom Barbados was dancing all unawares.

With a horrible crash the nation's number one newscaster fell with a sickening plop into a descending avalanche of multi-coloured jellies and then, finally, lay still as the band struck up the *Celebrity Squares* Tango.

Anna stood aghast.

Was this the man she had loved so passionately?

Was this the man — the thought hovered like a perilous butterfly in her mind — was this the man that she *still* loved?

CHAPTER VIII

The islands of Venice came into view beneath the wing of the DC10 like a patchwork quilt in a glistening sea.

Anna could just make out the famous silhouette of the Sistine Chapel, its bronzed horses glowing proudly in the autumn sunshine.

"Fasten your seat-belts, ladies and gentlemen," came the announcement over the tannoy. "We shall be arriving in Venice in approximately five minutes."

Anna looked to her side where her husband-to-be had fallen asleep over a copy of *Now!* magazine. His mouth lay open and cigarette ash stained the front of his cream-coloured jacket.

Not for the first time she felt her heart hardening against him.

John Snargs. Everybody said they were the perfect match. A handsome couple. And indeed he was handsome.

But how could they guess her inner secret, the true reason why she had announced to the world her plans to marry?

How could they know that it was Ronnie Beaujolais she really loved and

that her engagement to another man had been no more than a desperate, foolhardy attempt to provoke Ronnie to jealousy, so forcing him, she hoped, to declare his love for her?

The love she knew he harboured behind his mask of rough indifference.

How could she have foreseen the long bitter strike that kept Ronnie out of her reach for many weeks?

Now the time had come to bring an end to her little game. Whatever she felt about John — and looking at him now, snoring loudly at her side, his body sprawled unattractively in his seat, she knew it was not love — she had nonetheless to tell him the truth.

*　　*　　*

A Thomson Autumn-Break in Venice had been his idea.

And if only things had been otherwise she would have relished being in the world's famous City of Love.

As she looked out of her bedroom window onto the twinkling lights of the Grand Canal, she could hear below the sound of happy strolling lovers and pigeons cooing like a million violins.

"You look tired," John said, casually slipping an arm around her petite, perfectly formed waist. "Why don't we make an early night of it?"

It was odd. It should have been so perfect. In Venice of all places. Yet she felt a cold shudder run down her spine. Her heart felt like ice.

"Not now," she said, trying not to sound unfriendly. "Why don't we go for a ride in a gondola? I feel a bit tense after the flight."

He lit a cigarette moodily, blowing the smoke through his nostrils.

"Okey dokey," he sighed, looking at his watch. "I could do with a drink."

*　　*　　*

Water lapped the side of the black gondola as Anna gazed in wonder at the passing pageant of history.

It was like a picture from her schoolroom days brought to life before her eyes.

Behind them a cheery Venetian in a striped apron and red hat sang in a deep baritone his ancient melody of love.

Now she had to tell him, that was clear. And what would be the point of holding back?
"John. . . " she began, but the words wouldn't come.

It was going to be harder than she had imagined. Her perfectly formed heart beat faster and faster. If only *he* was there.

And then suddenly their peace was shattered by the sound of shouting and the shrill wailing of a police siren.

As they rounded the corner of the canal, a confused scene met her perfectly formed eyes. An excited crowd had gathered at the water's edge. Someone was being pulled out of the water.

"What's up, Musso?" John asked, turning to the gondolier, his reporter's nose scenting a story.

The Venetian shrugged. "Issa nothing," he laughed. "The crazy Englishman is fallen offa the bridge again. Too mucha vino! Too mucha vino!"

He winked and laughed heartily as they drew alongside.

It was then that Anna noticed a familiar object floating past her in the water. It looked like a bird's nest upside-down.

She looked down and read the tell-tale name crudely printed in biro on the label of the toupee: "RONNIE BEAUJOLAIS"

"John," she said firmly, in a voice she scarcely recognised. "There's something very important I think you ought to know. . . "

CHAPTER IX

T
he Inter-City 125 flashed past the untidy backs of suburban terraced houses on its way into Paddington. Anna looked at her watch, as did the commuters around her. It was still early and she would be in plenty of time.

Her weekend at the huge country mansion of the Somerset landowner Sir Auberon Waugh had done much to ease the ache in her perfectly formed heart.

There had been lavish banqueting in the panelled Georgian dining room. Riding with hounds through the golden November countryside. A Masked Ball in the Old Coachhouse with the host playing the part of Mr Pickwick and herself as Nell Gwynne.

It had been a delightful interlude which had oh too quickly come to an end.

Anna sighed deeply and gathered up her crocodile-skin suitcases and the bulging hamper of freshly cured venison pate and home-grown figs thrust on her at the last minute by her ebullient host.

Tonight she was News-At-Tenning. And he would be there, the man whose very name had the power to plunge her into a whirlpool of conflicting passions — Ronnie, oh Ronnie!

Would there ever be an end to the waiting?

How long was eternity?

Anna tipped the cabbie and walked briskly into ITN House past the saluting commissionaire.

"Good morning, Mr Coren," she cried, her perfectly formed lips breaking into a smile.

"Nice weekend, Miss?" the beaming functionary queried as Anna sped on her way towards the newscasters' room on the second floor, down the long carpeted corridor with numbered doors on either side.

It was then, as she drew near the office of the Controller, Sir Julian Hetherington, that she heard the sound of angry voices.

"We've had enough, d'you hear me?" came Sir Julian's military bark. "What you do in private's your own affair but the company can't stand any more. You're fired, d'you hear me? Fired!! Fired!!!"

Anna hurried on, her heart trembling with foreboding. Who could it be whimpering — for she could hear

∗   ∗   ∗

whimpering — on the other side of the door? Some luckless technician, perhaps. They were always coming in late and getting into trouble.

*   *   *

"And in Part Two — Sir Geoffrey Howe spells it out to British Steel. Prince Andrew goes jogging with the Girl Guides. And why Harry the Moose won't be going home for Christmas — Join us again after the break."

The air was electric. She had never known Ronnie so agitated. His war wound was clearly much worse, and the long weeks of leisure during the strike had plainly taken their toll.

Again and again during the film sequences he had taken long draughts from his medicine bottle. His face was the colour of a beetroot and Penny from Make-Up was now busy dabbing powder on his flushed brow.

Desperately, she wanted to steady him, to take away the pain. And yes, those were tears streaking down the war veteran's creased cheeks.

Twice he stumbled as he described how a fire had raged through a Glasgow warehouse. And again when it came to the familiar phrase — "Snow ploughs were out at dawn" — the world's Number One newscaster fluffed his lines.

Then a most extraordinary thing happened. As she recited "Here are the main points again", Ronnie leaned across and thrust a dog-eared envelope into her perfectly formed hand.

Then he was gone. Before even the News At Ten theme had thundered triumphantly towards its climactic end.

She looked about her. But there was no sign of him. Only in the distance could she hear the familiar clanking sound of his pathetic plastic carrier bag.

The studio lights dimmed and the large room was suddenly deserted.

Still sitting at the famous desk, Anna tore open the envelope with trembling hands.

She read, at first silently and then — she knew not why — out loud:

Dear Old Bean,
This is Goodbye.
Ever since you came into my life, my days and nights have been a torment.
You know me, old girl. I'm not much of a one for putting things into words, not like some of the pretty boys around this place.
I fell for you, hook line and sinker. But I knew it could never be. I could never hope to live up to your high expectations.
That's why it's best I go now. Don't believe the lies in the papers. Only you will know the real reason.
If I don't do it now I could easily find myself turning to drink just to forget you.
Don't try to find me. It will only make matters worse for
Your old News At Ten chum,
Ronnie.

The tears welled up in Anna's large perfectly formed eyes and cascaded down her cheeks, down onto the crumpled writing paper where the ink ran into a blue lake.

Up in the gallery two technicians roared with coarse laughter.

She had not been alone after all. But what did it matter now — now that her love had gone?

——— THE END ———

Motoring Information

Tonight's lighting-up time 18.53
Owing to faulty traffic lights at the Hogarth Roundabout, the gentleman who normally deals with this one is un-avoidably delayed. For further details, go for a drive and see for yourself.

Weather

TODAY'S WEATHER

Reykavik	14⁰
Helsinki	2⁰
Torremolinos	21⁰
Ulan Bator	8⁰
Neasden	6⁰
Port Now	7⁰

Further Outlook: For details see your TV Weather Service.

Magazines

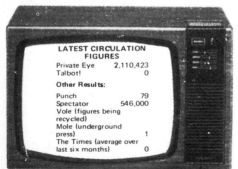

LATEST CIRCULATION FIGURES

Private Eye	2,110,423
Talbot!	0

Other Results:

Punch	79
Spectator	546,000
Vole (figures being recycled)	
Mole (underground press)	1
The Times (average over last six months)	0

Vital inf
at your fing
Gnom

The scientific data discovery of the century! For a mere £9,999.99 you can now convert your TV set into a 24-hour-a-day Communications Power House thanks to Gnomefax, the revolution in micro-chip media processing. It's incredible!

The Gnomefax System is a must for:

- o executives
- o motorists
- o housewives
- o sportsmen
- o students
- o social workers

Recipes

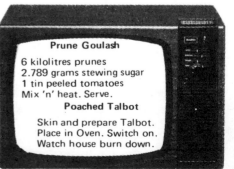

Prune Goulash

6 kilolitres prunes
2.789 grams stewing sugar
1 tin peeled tomatoes
Mix 'n' heat. Serve.

Poached Talbot

Skin and prepare Talbot. Place in Oven. Switch on. Watch house burn down.

A GOVERNMENT WARNING

LONDON IN DANGER!

At any moment between now and 1982, large parts of London could be submerged under a flood of magazines. Millions could die. It could be the worst disaster of modern times — unless action is taken now to alert the public to the danger that faces the capital.

The threat comes from literally hundreds of millions of unsold copies of the news magazine *Talbot!* which are piling up in warehouses, newsagents and disused bomb shelters all over London.

At any moment, experts predict, the sheer weight of the magazines could prove so great that they would spill out in a tidal wave, engulfing whole streets and communities without warning.

If you live in a *Talbot!* risk area you should prepare now for a possible emergency.

1. All householders in these areas should sandbag their houses to a height of fourteen feet (3.61482 metres). They should also cover their windows with brown paper, and lay in vast quantities of tinned salmon, marmite and other essential foodstuffs.

2. As the threat approaches, sirens will sound and special emergency broadcasts will be made on all news-media. All those living in high-risk areas should retire at this point to an upper floor and await the worst.

3. The final danger sign will come when huge cracks begin to appear in warehouses, and it becomes impossible to enter your local newsagent for the vast piles of unsold issues of *Talbot!*.

Shortly afterwards you will hear a series of dull thuds and booms. You will see a vast river of magazines coming round the corner of your street and flowing towards you like molten lava. Do not approach the magazines as you could easily be crushed to death.

DO NOT HAVE A GO. DO NOT PANIC. THE GOVERNMENT HAS EVERYTHING UNDER CONTROL.

Issued by the Department of the Environment

"You've done it now, David – Here comes his mother!"

New relevant prayers proposed for C.of E.

by Our Religious Affairs Correspondent
CLIFFORD LONGFORD

Following the Bishop of Winchester's initiative *(see above)*, a new set of prayers, "more in tune with current life-styles", is to be introduced into the *Series 94 Alternative Prayer Book*, at present being drawn up by an inter-denominational committee under the chairmanship of the Bishop of Neasden, The Rt. Rev. Alexander Mugabe.

Apart from the Bishop himself, the committee consists of three men with beards, a woman, and a black person. Its Literary Advisor is the well-known playwright, Lord Willis of Chislehurst.

A practising atheist, Lord Willis admits that he is "a regular non-attender" at his local church, but he defends his role on the panel by saying that "atheists have their views as well about the things that really matter".

Post-abortion prayer

A prayer for use after abortion has been composed by the Bishop of Winchester, Dr John Taylor, who wants it to be included in the new Alternative Services Book, due to be published in 1980. He does not consider the prayer amounts to approval of abortion or support for the law

These are some of the draft prayers at present under consideration:

Prayer For An A.I.D. Donor

O Lord, who promised Abraham that his seed would go forth and multiply, look with favour on the contents of this sterilised glass container. Wheresoever thou decidest it shalt go, in consultation with the local Health Authorities, let my spermatazoa play a constructive part in building a better society, in which all thy children can play a meaningful role and not get involved in conflict situations.

Amen

A Mugger's Prayer

O Lord, look down upon thy servant, M−− or N−−, and recognise that in doin' over this old lady, and pinchin' her pension money out of 'er 'andbag, I was merely expressin' my feelings of frustration at being a victim of an underprivileged environment. You yourself, who done over the money-changers, will I am sure totally understand my feelings at this moment in time.

Amen

Prayer For A Pregnant Unmarried Headmistress

O Lord, who yourself came into the world as a member of a one-parent family, safeguard we pray the rights of working women to fulfil themselves in their private lives in any way they want, without the interference of angry parents, self-righteous education authorities and interfering ITN reporters.

A-persons

TEST MATCH Special

(Men laughing)

BRIAN JOHNSON: Ha, ha, ha. That reminds me of a lunch I once had in Karachi. We all had to bring our own papadums.

(General laughter)

FRED TRUEMAN: Aye, I remember that story. I was once doing an interview with Herbert Sutcliffe — one of the all-time greats was our Herbert — bloody marvellous.

TREVOR BAILEY: They used to say that he grew the biggest cauliflowers in the West Riding. . .

JOHN ARLOTT: Well, that may be so, but down in my part of the country we all remember Farmer White's cauliflowers — and his broccoli. I wouldn't mind betting that old J.C. White's cauliflowers would have carried off all the prizes.

VOICE IN BACKGROUND: I think you'll find that Dennis Brookes of Northampton-shire grew a cauliflower weighing 48lbs 12oz during the 1938-39 tour of South Africa.

ARLOTT: Thank you, Bill.

TRUEMAN: Talking of cauli-flowers reminds me of a story Max Miller used to tell about a vicar and a veget-able marrow. . .

BRIAN JOHNSON *(nervously)*: Ha. Ha. Ha. I don't think we can have that one, Freddie — not if it's the one I'm thinking of.

FRED: Just as well, Brian, I've forgotten t'bugger!

BAILEY: If I can change the subject, I was talking to a chap over lunch who was saying that he was on the train from Leeds to Weston-super-Mare the other day, and. . .

JOHNSON: I'm sorry, I've got to interrupt you there, Trevor, because we've just got the latest news from Wimbledon which is that it's still raining.

ARLOTT: Wonderful thing, the British weather, isn't it? No one day is like another.

VOICE IN BACKGROUND: That's not strictly true, John. My records show that there

have now been seventeen days continuous rain, and that hasn't happened in June since 1890.

ARLOTT: Thank you, Bill. It reminds me of some lines by that great old Hampshire-man, E.B. Parsons:
'God gave to man the
     gift of rain,
He also gave the sun.
But if you must choose
     betwixt the twain,
The latter is more fun.'

(Laughter)

JOHNSON: I was down talking to the boys at Soddingham the other day, and the chaplain told me — awfully nice chap, the chaplain — they gave me an awfully good lunch — roast beef, cauliflower. . .

TRUEMAN: Excuse me, gents, I'm off to t'toilet.

VOICE IN BACKGROUND: That makes it the thirty-seventh time since lunch. . .

(Contd. 94 kHz)

MONTY PYTH

FLY

D

Part 94

<u>What Happens When We Are Bored To</u>
<u>Death And Sick At The Same Time.</u>

A Doctor Explains:
Dr Who-style music:

(Dr Jonathan is discovered seated in a gondola on the Grand Canal, Venice)

DOCTOR: In 1798 Jean-Jacques Galbraith invented the egg-timer. It was a revolutionary concept which changed not only the cooking of eggs, but man's whole view of himself. In fact, Galbraith can be called the Columbus of the Urinary Tract.

(X-Ray Film of Greater Intestine absorbing Scotch Egg)

DOCTOR: The stomach is like an enormous lift-shaft. What comes up must go down. When we swallow a Maltezer we take a conscious decision which affects the whole of our relationship with our environment.

(Close-up picture of enormous palpitating lump of flesh. Millions of viewers faint)

DOCTOR *(eating eclair)*: A cream-cake like this has much the same effect on our body as the D-Day invasion had on Europe. As it travels down the

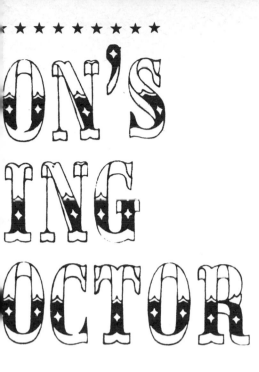

★ ★ ★ ★ ★ ★ ★ ★ ★

mighty Amazon of the lower oeso-
phagus, it is attacked by hundreds of
foreign bodies in field-grey Wehrmacht
uniforms.

(Cut to film of Hitler reviewing troops. Picture of surgeon plunging knife into huge, palpitating piece of flesh. Blood gushes out. Millions more viewers faint)

DOCTOR *(smiling and waving arms about)*: When we watch a programme like this, we may make a conscious decision to become sick. We can measure what happens with the help of this swingometer.

(Walks over to Prof. MacKenzie's enormous device, painted red, white and blue)

DOCTOR: Any piece of film showing blood gushing out of huge palpitating pieces of flesh can be given points under four headings: Squeamishness,
Embarrassment, Rage and what we doctors call P.P.S. — Prolonged Premature Sleep. Here, for example, is a man eating a Scotch Egg.

(Large picture of portly magazine proprietor consuming aforesaid viand)

DOCTOR: What happens if he makes a conscious decision to eat a Maltezer at the same time? The effect, as we can see from this X-Ray film of the uncharted wastes of the Semi-Colon, is rather like what happens to the sewers of Calcutta after the monsoon has broken.

(Picture of H. Keswick being carted off to hospital)

DOCTOR: This man has now taken a conscious decision to become unconscious. The problem is — how can he tell his doctor what he thinks is wrong with him? It is rather like the problem which faces a man watching television when he wants to indicate that a particular programme makes him feel sick, enraged and bored all at the same time. He can't shout at the screen. Or rather, he can, but no one will hear him.

CAST

A Doctor . . . . . . *Harpo Marx*
The Greater Intestine . *Lord Goodman*
The Lower Intestine . . *Bryan Forbes*
Comic Surgeon *James Robertson-Justice*
Nurse . . . . . . *Barbara Windsor*
H. Keswick . . . . . *Robert Morley*
Man on Slab . . . . . . *David Frost*

"We call her Melody. She lingers on"

ffolkes

TEN TO WATCH IN THE 80's

Nigel Wheatcroft, 47. Newly-elected Tory MP, he is widely regarded as the most promising member of the 'Class of '79'A passionate moderate and committed European, Wheatcroft was at Eton and Somerville. Currently P.P.S. to Sir Hector Strames.

WHO ARE the men and women who are going to make the news in the Britain of the '80s? This *Observer* guide tells you who to watch out for in the headlines of tomorrow.

Cynthia Stargs, 25. After a brilliant Double First at Christ Church, she has become the hottest thing in the Civil Service since Dame Cecil Sharp.

Currently working as Deputy Principal Researcher to the Central Co-ordinating Advisory Unit, she is widely tipped for top honours.

Annunciata Starborgling, 19. The most brilliant lady cricketer Britain has seen for decades, she could well succeed Ian Botham as Captain of the England team.

Rev J.C. Flannel, 56. Controversial, hard-hitting author of *Jesus — The Biggest Hoax In History*, Flannel is widely tipped as next Archbishop of Canterbury.

L ibby Horseface, 21. A tireless campaigner for women's rights and abortion reform, Libby (currently chief spokesperson for SAM — 'Shoot All Men') is likely to make a big mark in the '80s.

H orace Mole, 49. Brilliant prize-winning Cambridge historian, widely tipped to become next Vice-Chancellor of Neasden University. A 'neo-Marxist', his latest book on the economic causes of the Balkan War of 1836 fluttered the academic dove-cotes.

S ir Peter Jaybotham, 49. Brilliant Double First at Lady Margaret Hall, Sir Peter is widely regarded as 'the ablest ex-Ambassador in the business'. Could become next Secretary-General of UN.

F rank Johnson, 43. Brilliant iconoclastic journalist, widely tipped to become a regular columnist on *Talbot!* magazine.

S onia Gladbundle, 21. Currently working as a tea-shop waitress in Wigan, Lancs, she is widely tipped to become the next Angela Rippon.

R on Hall, 56. Brilliant iconoclastic journalist, he is widely tipped to become Director-General of the BBC in succession to Simon Jenkins.

CHAPTER ONE

A THIN WIND ruffled the few remaining leaves on the pavement of Bedford Square. It looked like rain. In the fifth-floor office, looking out over the rooftops, two men sat staring at a pile of papers.

"It's no good, Hodder," one of them said finally. "The old firm is on the skids."

Hodder sat playing abstractedly with a paper-clip. A gust of rain brushed against the window. His thoughts strayed back to New College lawn thirty years before. A girl in a white dress. The distant click of croquet balls. The sun shining on warm Cotswold stone.

Things had seemed promising then. How could he have known that it would end like this? Sitting in a down-at-heel publisher's office in Bloomsbury, a bit fatter, thin on top, too much alimony.

Stoughton shifted in his chair and stared again at the figures that had come through from Accounts. Whichever way you looked at them they told the same story.

Another gust of wind swept across the square, but Hodder's thoughts were elsewhere. Soon it would be 12.15 — time for lunch at the Garrick. Murgatroyd would probably be there. He usually was on Tuesdays.

'Le Carre picked his teeth abstractedly...'

CHAPTER TWO

THE TELEPHONE rang by Le Carre's bed. He had been awake for hours, staring at the ceiling. He was washed up and he knew it. He hadn't had a new idea in years. He should never have left the Office.

It had been easy then. Scribbling away before breakfast. An hour snatched at the typewriter before some boring diplomatic reception. Five thousand words a week had seemed child's play in those days.

Who was ringing him? It could be Melvyn Barg, offering another interview on the South Bank Show. What was the point? He had nothing new to say.

He picked up the receiver.

"Yes?" he said, after a long pause.

So it was Hodder. It had been a long time. They had last met in Frankfurt. Staying together at the Hotel Weidenfeld. Murgatroyd had been there. He usually went over for the Book Fair.

"Le Carre," said Hodder. "We need you. There's a job. No one else can do it except you."

Outside the rain beat a faint tattoo on the window pane. Le Carre picked his teeth abstractedly.

"You're talking to the wrong man," he said. "I'm finished with all that."

His thoughts strayed to Cynthia. Why had she left him? Could it be because he was so boring? Or was she in love with Murgatroyd?

Hodder was speaking again. "I've been talking it over with Stoughton." He spoke excitedly. "There's a train to Paddington at 3.15. We'll get a car to meet you. We count on you, John. . . "

CHAPTER THREE

THE OFFICE hadn't changed much. The same handful of remaindered titles gathering dust on the shelves. A gust of rain beat at the window, but Le Carre remained unaware of it.

The four men were sitting round a table. Hodder, looking a little greyer. Stoughton, thinning on top. And a young man Le Carre had never met before.

"Do you know Cohen?" Hodder enquired.

Le Carre mumbled a conventional greeting.

"Cohen will be handling your operation," Hodder went on. "It'll be a piece of cake."

In the ashtray on the table was a pile of cigarette stubs. They looked as if they'd been there for a month. Le Carre was still wondering why the Old Firm wanted him back so badly.

The young man began to explain: "Mr Le Carre," he said, "you remember the Tinker, Tailor affair?"

It had long been a legend in the firm. Le Carre's finest hour. A gust of wind ruffled the trees outside, as the spy-novelist's thoughts went back to the moment when he had first seen his name at the top of the best-seller lists. How unreal it all seemed now.

"Well, it's come up again," Cohen went on. "The BBC have bought it. It

'Don't worry about a plot...'

looks like being the biggest thing since Edward and Mrs Simpson. They've even got Alec Guinness. It can't miss."

So this is what they were leading up to, Le Carre thought. They want to cash in.

"We want to cash in," said Hodder. "It's as simple as that. You can do it in your sleep, old man. Just write anything that comes into your head — Russkies, Berlin Wall, all that sort of stuff. Absolutely down your street. Don't worry about plot or anything complicated like that. Just get the words down and we'll do the rest. We'll put your name big on the cover, print 100,000 in hardback and we'll all be ahead of the game again."

"That's it," said Stoughton. "It's a winner. What do you say?"

Le Carre remained silent. His thoughts were already at work. An old Russian woman waiting for a bus in a Parisian street. A corpse on Hampstead Heath. A tie-up with the KGB. But where did Murgatroyd come in?

That was the real question.

World Copyright Le Carre Syndications Ltd. Grand Bahama.

To The Editor of The Daily Telegraph

Rural Preparations For Third World War

From Sir Herbert Gussett

SIR,—Recent world events have brought home to us as never before the very real possibility of a Third World War. Today Afghanistan, tomorrow — who knows? It cannot surely be long before the Russian hordes have swept across Europe like a forest fire, and the nuclear rockets are cascading around us like a shower of hailstones.

Many of your readers will have been appalled to learn from your columns that our present government has apparently no plans whatever to deal with this eventuality. Let them, however, take heart. In at least one remote corner of this once-great country, I wish the world to know that there are still those of us who have been taking active steps to ensure that, when the holocaust comes, Britain can take it.

Last Thursday evening, at an Extraordinary General Meeting of the ——————— (name deleted for security reasons) Parish Council, a number of us got together at the Lamb & Flag to set up a Special Ad-Hoc Emergency Committee to coordinate field operations in the event of World War Three breaking out.

PHASE ONE:

It was unanimously resolved that one of our number should be detailed to read the *Daily Telegraph* each morning, on a page-to-page basis, to give us a constant up-date on the world situation. Just as soon as a world-war-type crisis seems imminent, we move onto Phase Two.

PHASE TWO:

Members of the Committee, working on a shift basis, will mount a round-the-clock monitoring operation on BBC news bulletins. On hearing the actual announcement from Number Ten that World War Three has been declared, the final Top Secret Phase of our plan will move into operation.

PHASE THREE (FOR YOUR EYES ONLY):

1. Key personnel will assemble on the-double at Map Reference 30Z 9GT (Lamb & Flag). Wives regrettably cannot be included owing to lack of shelter facilities.

2. Key personnel will proceed directly to shelter situation (i.e. cellar of Lamb & Flag). (Key in Drambuie bottle by till.)

3. The following are deemed 'Key Personnel' who alone will be permitted to enter the 'restricted area':

Lt-Col "Buffy" Frobisher MG, GCMN.

H. Gussett

M. Balon (landlord of Lamb & Flag).

4. Since we cannot at this moment in time foresee the exact duration of hostilities, radiation dangers etc, the Committee has taken top-secret steps to ensure that the Nuclear Shelter Area is equipped with all necessary life-support systems to last for an indefinite period — to wit:

48 cases McHackey's Very Old Finest Malt-Style Whisky;

Ditto Gin, Brandy etc.;

80 Firkins "Khyber Pass" Export Stout;

8 packets 'Spearmint Flavour' Crisps;

2 bags Nuts 'n' Raisins.

5. At the moment when the 'All-Clear' is sounded (or supplies run out, whichever is the sooner), the key personnel will emerge to establish friendly relations with the enemy.

Useful words here (culled from the BBC's invaluable series 'From Russia With Love') I regret that, for security reasons, these are omitted.

6. Let the message go out loud and clear. We are ready for anything Johnnie Russkie chooses to throw at us. Mrs Thatcher may do her worst. But one thing is for certain. In this neck of the woods at least, there'll always be an England.

Yours,

H. GUSSETT
(Hon. Field-Marshal),
The Bunker,
Somewhere in
Southern England,
Dorset.

PS. For security reasons I would be grateful if you would not print this letter.

THE G
BOOK OF

The most influential thinker in the history of the world, Albert Einstein, was born a hundred years ago today. His theories turned the world upside down. Thanks to him we now know that even the statement 'Einstein was born a hundred years ago' is, strictly speaking, meaning-less. Now, in a unique symposium, some of the world's leading experts explain for the first time, in easy-to-understand layman's language, just what the old bore was on about.

Contributors include:

DR. JONATHAN MILLER, SIR PETER MEDAWAR, NEILS BORE, GEORGE STEINER, a lot of men called HUXLEY, PETER USTINOV, BRIAN REDHEAD, H.R.H. PRINCE CHARLES, PROF. RONALD DWORKIN and many others.

WHAT YOU WILL LEARN

When you open this book you will enter a new dimension, where time and space assume a new meaning. Just imagine that you are on a train to Basingstoke travelling at 90 mph. Where are you? Wherever you are is irrelevant. The fact of the matter is, as Einstein explained, if you throw a cricket ball out of the window, you are demonstrating in a crucial way how the universe operates.

Let us put it another way:

Your watch says the time is 4.15. If another man in Australia looks at his watch simultane-ously, owing to the curvature of the space-time continuum, he will see that it is only 4.14 and 59.6220712 seconds, and that the water in his bath is spiralling out in an anti-clockwise direction.

Einstein was the first man not only to penetrate these mysteries, but to reduce them to simple, easy-to-follow formulae.

NOME EINSTEIN

In his classic equation $2 + 2$ = nearly 4 (depending on where you are), this towering genius overthrew all hitherto accepted versions of the way the universe works.

★Did you know that the light you switch on in your front room may already be out by the time its rays reach Jupiter? And that if your front garden was to turn into a black hole, it would suck in the entire universe in a matter of seconds, thus entitling you to a rent rebate?

These are just some of the amazing, easy-to-grasp facts which spill in a never-ending stream from the 4,000-plus pages of the Ein Book of Gnomestein.

★ One of the greatest misconceptions about Einstein is that his theories were not relevant to everyday life. In fact, every time you pick up a toothbrush you are proving one of Einstein's theories — that everything connects with everything else.

Another misconception swept away is that Einstein was just another head-in-the-clouds boffin. In fact he had his feet on the ceiling just like everyone else.

✸ **FACT:** Despite his giant intelligence, he was unable to remember his own telephone number.

✸ **FACT:** Einstein was against war. On many occasions, he confided to his friends, "War is a bad thing." And yet, in 1939, he invented the hydrogen bomb.

✸ **FACT:** In common with many of the world's greatest geniuses — e.g. Sherlock Holmes and Yehudi Menuhin — Einstein knew no better way of relaxing than playing the violin.

✸ **FACT:** Einstein could have been one of the richest men in the world yet he died penniless.

✸ **FACT:** Einstein trained bluebottles to form a jazz band.

✸ **FACT:** These facts have gone on too long *(W. Deedesh)*.

PLUS:

Life Beyond the Grave: does it exist? Einstein reveals for the first time that death in itself is a misnomer. "We do not die, as such, We merely explode outwards in a series of minute particles." *(See diagram of Lord Goodman, p. 408)*

ALSO in the Gnome Book of Stein:
✸ The Giant Bee of Stonehenge — at last the truth about Druidical marriage rites.

<u>Plus:</u> FREE 3-D Specs with each volume purchased before March last year.

Read what these famous people said about the Gnome Book of Stein:

Sir Golly Jamstein, industrialist: *Once and for all, it proved to me that the Oxo Cube is perfectly round.*

Bill Grundy, broadcaster: *Once and for all, it proved to me that the quickest way back from the pub is not a shtraight line.*

William Toadthrush Jr., expert on Middle-Eastern affairs: *Once and for all, this mighty tasteful volume proved to me that what goes down doesn't have to come up. Hic!*

Rush TODAY to buy this book before Einstein's theories are disproved.

NAME . . . .

ADDRESS . . . .

. . . .

Send cheque for £417 + p&p.

TV
CRUX OF DECISION

INTRODUCED BY

Ludicrous Kennedy

NUMBER 6:

The strange case of Wally Oblomov

KENNEDY *(putting on glasses)*: On June 6th 1973 this man *(shot of balding man in pyjamas)* took a decision which was to change his life. He decided to go to bed and stay there.

For most people that would have been the end of the matter. But not for Wally Oblomov.

In this, the first of two programmes, we look at the repercussions of Mr Oblomov's strange change of life-style on his family, his neighbours, his local community helpers, the meals-on-wheels service, social workers, the local social security office, the DHSS snoopers, and the team of sociologists from nearby Dollis Hill University who for the past six years have been working on a special study of the man they call 'the Bed Man of Neasden'.

KENNEDY *(standing outside council house)*: It was here, seven years ago, that neighbours first began to notice that something had changed in the day-to-day life-style of Wally Oblomov.

MRS SNARGS *(Caption — Neighbour)*: I came home from work one night and then I noticed all these milk bottles outside Mr Oblomov's door. There was about a week's worth. So I called out to him through the letter-box, "Mr Oblomov, are you alright?" And he just says, "I'm in bed". That's all he'd say. So I tells my husband and he says, "We'd better get the social workers round."

KENNEDY: What you are about to see is a filmed reconstruction of the events which followed.

(Interior of office in Neasden Town Hall. Man with beard is sitting at desk. Phone rings)

MAN WITH BEARD: Hullo, Mildew here. Yes. . . yes. . . yes. . . I see. . . yes. . . I see. . . yes. . . thank you very much. We'll see what we can do. *(Presses buzzer.)* Cathy, could you come in for a moment, please?

(Enter dumpy woman with beard and glasses)

KENNEDY VOICE-OVER: Fred Mildew, Chief Co-Ordinating Social Welfare Executive Officer, calls in one of his Pastoral Field Officers, Ms Pettigrew, to talk through the situation as he sees it.

MILDEW *(speaking in low, mono-tonous drone)*: Cathy, we've got a bit of a problem-situation here. It appears that a Mr Oblomov, of 103 Frank Soskice House down there on the Tesco Road Estate, has decided to remain in an in-bed situation for an indefinite period. That is all the data we have on the client at this moment in time. I want you to investigate and produce a report so that we can get an evaluation of the problem. Perhaps we could have a meeting on this one at a later stage.

KENNEDY: Two months later Ms Pettigrew went round to see Oblomov. Our cameras were there.

(Scene of grotty council flat. Man in bed)

MS PETTIGREW *(speaking in low, monotonous drone)*: I see from your file, Mr Oblomov, that you have now been in bed for three months and four days. Apparently you're not ill. There's nothing physically wrong with you. But you do have this problem, don't you, of not wanting to get out of bed? Now, it's nothing to be ashamed of, Mr Oblomov. It's quite normal to want to opt out if we feel for any reason unable to cope with day-to-day situations. Would you say depression was a factor? I mean, there's nothing abnormal about depression.

KENNEDY: The following week Ms Pettigrew made her report. As a result, a meeting was called to con-sider Mr Oblomov's case from every angle.

(Cut to twelve men and women with beards sitting round long table, all speaking in low, monotonous drones)

FIRST SOCIAL WORKER: Now we move on to Case No. 312A/47B, Mr Oblomov. You've all read the reports on this one.

REG HAMMERSMITH *(Caption — Chief Welfare Co-Ordinating Officer)*: Barry, could we have the psychiatric evaluation on this one?

SECOND MAN WITH BEARD: Well, looking at the reports, according to the latest up-date we have here, which you'll find in Para 87(b) under Section 41. . .

(All men with beards fumble in briefcases. Close-up of man lighting pipe in meaningful way)

. . . the position, as I see it, is this. The basic problem is essentially one of motivation, basically. Mr Oblomov, as I see it, is in bed. And what he refuses to do is get up. In other words, that is, put simply, what the situation is here. As I understand, all usual procedures have been followed in this case. E.g. Mr Oblomov is now in receipt of regular visits from social workers, the Meals-on-Wheels service, the Home-Help service, the In-Home Day Care service, and all other services laid down by the provisions of the 1975 Act. We have also advised Mr Oblomov that he is entitled to full Social Security Benefit, plus Supplementary Benefit, Rent Rebate, Rate Rebate, Fuel Allowance, TV Licence Rebate. . . anything I've left out here, Mrs Reddish?

GLORIA REDDISH *(for it is she)*: There is something I'd like to bring to the attention of the meeting — namely the question of Supple- mentary Supplementary Benefit, which would be allowable in this case, being a non-specific case where no deprivation as such has occurred, but where there is nevertheless a *prima facie* case of non-mobility

CRUX OF DECISION

which has not been caused through industrial accident or related causes. *(Everyone nods in agreement)*

KENNEDY: That was last September. Tonight in the studio we talk to Mr Oblomov in person.

(Oblomov is wheeled in, still in bed, by two male nurses)

KENNEDY *(taking off glasses)*: Mr Oblomov, we've heard your story from a number of experts, who will be joining us later for a studio discussion.

(Camera pans round studio full of 1000 men with beards, all paid for by us)

KENNEDY: But before we start, I'd just like to put to you one question. Why have you decided to stay in bed?

OBLOMOV *(with heavy wink)*: Well, I tell you, guv — with 280 quid comin' in each week, plus free meals, someone to clean the house, free telly, free copies of *Talbot!* etc. etc., would you bother to get up?

KENNEDY: So the tragic case of Mr Oblomov continues. In next week's Crux of Decision we ask: "What more can we do to help people like Wally Oblomov?"

DR. RUNCIBLE talks to KENNETH HARGS

WHAT is he like, the 57-year-old unknown ex-war hero who next month is rocketed into the CofE hot seat? Here, for the first time ever, Dr Ronald Runcible talks openly and frankly as he has never talked before about the great issues that are today perplexing the man in the street — women priests, gay clergy, wife-battering, one-parent families and all the rest of the claptrap you usually expect from Archbishops of Canterbury nowadays.

HARGS: Dr Nancy, I'd like to begin by asking you about this appalling wife you've got.

RUNCIBLE: I admit that, in a very real sense, she is the cross I have to bear. But of course one of the blessings I look forward to during my term of office is that I shall be seeing considerably less of her and her beastly piano.

HARGS: Dr Runcible, I would like to ask you what were your feelings when you first heard that you had been chosen to appear on the Michael Parginson Show?

DR RUNCIBLE: Well, I will confess that in a very real sense it was the hardest decision I have ever had to make in my life. My initial feeling was simply one of shock. But I prayed about it, and then I prayed again — and suddenly the answer came to me. It was a tremendous challenge that I could not afford to duck — on my salary!

HARGS: Ha, ha, ha, ha. Very good, Your Reverence. But I'd like to turn now, if I may, to the question that is worrying Christians probably more than any other. Should gay women priests be allowed to re-marry in Church?

RUNCIBLE: You know I've agonised over this one. . . probably more than any other issue. I think we have to go back to the fundamentals. It's awfully easy, isn't it? . . . on the one hand. . . on the other. . . Our Lord Himself. . . Cambodia. . . young people today. . . challenge of technology. . . pastoral outreach. . . moral confusion. . . interface of caring and sharing. . . Church's role . . . no easy answer.

HARGS: Dr Runcible, thank you very much.

"Who taught your kettle to swear like that?"

GEORGE BROWN — "Unreliable, tired, emotional, and often intoxicated."

WILSON — "Shifty, weak, incompetent — couldn't drive a no. 11 bus."

CALLAGHAN — "Weak, incompetent, shifty — couldn't box his way out of a paper-bag."

CROSSMAN — "Shifty, unreliable, rat-like cunning, leopard-skin accessories."

4 JULY 1967: Walked through St James's Park to Cabinet meeting. Two hours wrangling over what to do about the Nargs Report. I say 'do nothing'. Crossman puts foot in it as usual. In the end nothing decided.

7 FEBRUARY 1968: J. *[Joe Boggis — General Secretary of the Amalgamated National Union of Fish-Paste Operatives,* comes to see me about Nargs. He is very upset, and warns that he has not been consulted. I soothe him down, but then H. *[Sir Horace Chillblain — Permanent Under Secretary to the Department of Productivity]* blunders in and wrecks the whole thing. There's going to be big trouble with regard to this one.

Crisis Years

HEALEY — "Unreliable, arrogant, power-crazed, bushy eyebrows."

WEDGWOOD BENN —"Shifty, mad, power-crazed — he would shoot his own grandmother if given half a chance,"

THE AUTHOR — "Intensely able, brilliant grasp, only one who knew what was going on."

10 SEPTEMBER 1969: At last the whole Nargs fiasco is blown wide open. Huge headlines in morning papers — "WILSON FURIOUS OVER NARGS LEAK". Naturally I am blamed, although I know perfectly well that it was all a put-up job by Jim as part of his long-term plan to discredit Harold.

15 JUNE 1970: We have lost the election. It is just as I feared. Who is to blame? Harold, Jim, Denis, Roy, Dick, Barbara all played their part in this disaster. As far as I can see, I am the only one who foresaw everything and can take no responsibility.

NEXT WEEK: What Marcia really said to George — and the night Fred Peart said "I've had enough" and had to be taken home.

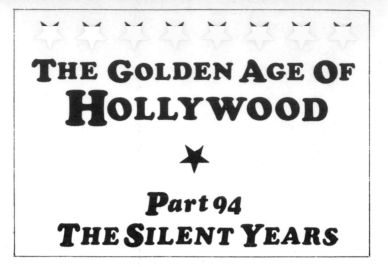

THE GOLDEN AGE OF HOLLYWOOD

★

Part 94
THE SILENT YEARS

JAMES MASON *(for it is he)*: In 1924 a penniless young Hungarian lens-grinder arrived in Beverly Hills with not more than a few dollars. His name was Andre B. Deutschberger. His impact on the infant motion picture industry was to be revolutionary.

94-YEAR-OLD HARRIDAN WITH ORANGE WIG, FACE-LIFT AND SMALL POODLE SITTING IN LAP: I remember the first time I ever set eyes on Andre. It was at a party given by George Schlumberger for his new star over at Fox, Ethel Mermanberger. Everyone was there — Charlie Schultzheimer, Eddie Duval, Gloria Heidelberg — she'd just finished *The Sheikh of Montmartre* with Rex Max and Irving Ingram.

MASON: In 1926, Deutschberger borrowed ten dollars from Waldo Puccini and began to shoot his now-legendary 300-reel epic, *How The Pyramids Were Made.*

(Scratched old film showing thousands of extras carrying cardboard stones across desert. Wagner-style music)

94-YEAR-OLD MAN IN COLOURFUL MIAMI BEACH SHIRT WITH FACE-LIFT: I was second cameraman to Hoagy Weinstock when Deutschberger made *Pyramids*. It was one hell of a show. Deutschberger never believed in scripts. I remember one day Jean Wimpy, who was playing Cleopatra, was literally in tears. She said, "Mr Deutschberger, what am I supposed to say?" Andre looked at her through his horn-rimmed spectacles and he just said: "Jean honey, they haven't invented the talkies yet — so you don't have to bother your pretty little head about things like that."

MASON: In 1928 Deutschberger became involved in the now-legendary battle between his own studio, Universal Colossal Pictures, and Ferdie de Talbot's Colossal Universal, over a new star, the young and then unknown Alice Facecloth.

Andre B. Deutschberger

94-YEAR-OLD CRONE WITH MAUVE HAIRPIECE AND DEAF-AID: I was a make-up artist with Universal Colossal the day Alice Facecloth walked into the studio. She hit everyone with a wham. She was definitely star material, and Deutschberger knew it. He at once cast her as Helen of Troy in *The Walls of Jericho*. This was the biggest biblical picture that had ever been made. It cost literally millions. Deutschberger shot the whole thing on location in the Arizona Desert.

(Very old film showing Queen Boadicea riding on chariot surrounded by Zulu warriors. Wagner-style music)

MASON: Then came disaster. With the coming of the talkies, Deutschberger's magic seemed to have left him. In 1930 he spent a fortune on a comedy film about the sinking of the Titanic called *The Iceberg Cometh*. It cost over 2 million dollars and starred the then-unknown Doald Trelford and Gloria Grundy. Embittered by the film's failure, Deutschberger shook the dust of Hollywood from his heels for ever.

NEXT WEEK: The Years Of Boredom.

The makers of this film would like to thank:
The National Film Archive of Canada
The Tokyo Museum of Motion Picture History
The Institute of Contemporary Cinematographic Arts, Neasden
The Library of Congress, Kabul
The Gulbenkian Foundation for Furthering the Advancement of Mankind
The Imperial Bore Museum

RESEARCHERS: Penny Farthing, Sue Grabbit, Bennie Green, Eddie Maxted, Ros Katzenellenbogen, Roger Graefe, Kevin Hemeling, Mike Trousers *(That's enough researchers — Ed)*.
PRODUCED, DEVISED, DIRECTED & WRITTEN BY Sid Bore.

✷ ✷ ✷ ✷ ✷ ✷ ✷ ✷ ✷ ✷ ✷ ✷ ✷

FOCUS ON FACT
DAVID FROST
By Barty Fenton and Stuart Harris

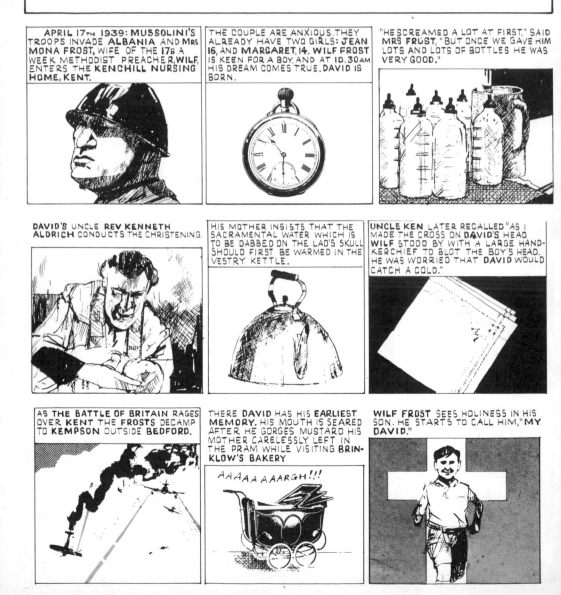

APRIL 17TH 1939: MUSSOLINI'S TROOPS INVADE ALBANIA AND MRS MONA FROST, WIFE OF THE 17& A WEEK METHODIST PREACHER, WILF, ENTERS THE KENCHILL NURSING HOME, KENT.

THE COUPLE ARE ANXIOUS. THEY ALREADY HAVE TWO GIRLS: JEAN 16, AND MARGARET, 14. WILF FROST IS KEEN FOR A BOY, AND AT 10.30 AM HIS DREAM COMES TRUE. DAVID IS BORN.

"HE SCREAMED A LOT AT FIRST," SAID MRS FROST, "BUT ONCE WE GAVE HIM LOTS AND LOTS OF BOTTLES HE WAS VERY GOOD."

DAVID'S UNCLE REV KENNETH ALDRICH CONDUCTS THE CHRISTENING.

HIS MOTHER INSISTS THAT THE SACRAMENTAL WATER WHICH IS TO BE DABBED ON THE LAD'S SKULL SHOULD FIRST BE WARMED IN THE VESTRY KETTLE.

UNCLE KEN LATER RECALLED "AS I MADE THE CROSS ON DAVID'S HEAD WILF STOOD BY WITH A LARGE HANDKERCHIEF TO BLOT THE BOY'S HEAD. HE WAS WORRIED THAT DAVID WOULD CATCH A COLD."

AS THE BATTLE OF BRITAIN RAGES OVER KENT THE FROSTS DECAMP TO KEMPSON OUTSIDE BEDFORD.

THERE DAVID HAS HIS EARLIEST MEMORY. HIS MOUTH IS SEARED AFTER HE GORGES MUSTARD HIS MOTHER CARELESSLY LEFT IN THE PRAM WHILE VISITING BRINKLOW'S BAKERY

AAAAA AAARGH!!!

WILF FROST SEES HOLINESS IN HIS SON. HE STARTS TO CALL HIM, "MY DAVID."

CAMBRIDGE – FROST HAS WON A STATE SCHOLARSHIP. HE INFORMS HIS TEARFUL MOTHER UPON TAKING LEAVE OF THEIR HOME: "I HAVE NO INTEREST IN AN ACADEMIC CAREER. I WANT TO BECOME A TV PERSONALITY.

MONA

AT CAMBRIDGE THE TASTES OF OUR HERO FROM A TEETOTAL METHODIST HOME UNDERGO A CHANGE. HE IS FREQUENTLY 'TIRED' AND LEAVES THE CITY WITHOUT SETTLING A SIXTY POUND BILL AT A WINE BAR IN KINGS PARADE.

PREVIOUSLY HIS FAVOURITE FOODS HAVE BEEN CORNFLAKES AND CRISPS. NOW HE FORMS CABAL, A CLUB FOR 'GOURMETS'.

FROST TAKES AN ACTIVE INTEREST IN THE FAMOUS CAMBRIDGE ACTING CLUB THE FOOTLIGHTS. ONE DAY HE IS SENT TO GREAT YARMOUTH TO ARRANGE THE PUBLICITY FOR A CONSERVATIVE CLUB CABARET FEATURING PETER COOK, JOHN BIRD, AND ELEANOR BRON.

TO THE SURPRISE OF ALL THE POSTERS SAY:

GREAT YARMOUTH C.C.
PRESENT
DAVID FROST
& THE FOOTLIGHTS

1961. FROST LEAVES CAMBRIDGE TO BECOME A TRAINEE FOR THE LONDON TELEVISION COMPANY, REDIFFUSION.

AFTER INITIAL SETBACKS, THERE COMES AT LAST A BREAKTHROUGH. FROST COMPERES A SERIES OF PROGRAMMES ABOUT THE LATEST DANCE CRAZE – THE TWIST. "EVEN TODAY" WRITES HIS BIOGRAPHER WALLACE REYBURN "THOSE TWIST PROGRAMMES STAY IN THE MIND OF ALL THOSE WHO HAPPENED TO SEE THEM."

1961 HERALDS THE SATIRE BOOM. AT THE FORTUNE THEATRE THE REVUE BEYOND THE FRINGE PLAYS TO PACKED HOUSES.

THE MAIN TALKING POINT IS PETER COOK'S BRILLIANT IMITATION OF THE PRIME MINISTER, HAROLD MACMILLAN.

AT THE BLUE ANGEL NIGHT CLUB MEANWHILE, ASTONISHED AUDIENCES FIND THE COMPLETELY UNKNOWN CABARET ARTISTE, DAVID FROST PERFORMING EXACTLY THE SAME ACT!

OFFERS OF ALL KINDS POUR IN TO THE SUCCESSFUL YOUNG **FROST.** HE STARTS A COLUMN IN THE **D. MAIL** AND **THE OBSERVER**

HE IS INVITED TO DO A SUMMER SEASON AT **WESTON-SUPER-MARE**

BUT ONE PROJECT—A BOOK ON THE **DUTCH RESISTANCE**—REMAINS UNWRITTEN TO THIS DAY!

FROST MOVES FROM HIS **VICTORIA** DIGS TO A PLUSH **REGENCY HOUSE** IN **EGERTON CRESCENT.**

HE DECORATES IT WITH MANY PAINTINGS INCLUDING A **BRATBY.**

ON HIS DESK IS AN **AMERICAN** *GEO-CHRON* CLOCK SHOWING WHERE THE SUN IS SHINING IN THE WORLD AT ANY TIME.

FROST COMES UNDER FIRE FROM COLLEAGUES FOR THE WAY HE USES OTHER PEOPLE'S MATERIAL. **JONATHAN MILLER** STYLES HIM *"THE BUBONIC PLAGIARIST".*

ANOTHER CRITIC IS **PETER LEWIS,** AUTHOR OF A SKETCH ABOUT **HILTON HOTELS.**

FROST PERFORMS THE SKETCH IN COUNTLESS APPEARANCES ALL OVER THE WORLD. BUT **LEWIS** DOES NOT RECEIVE A PENNY.

ONE DAY THE **TW3** STUDIOS WERE VISITED BY THE CELEBRITY PANEL OF THE BBC'S POP SHOW, JUKE BOX JURY.

"I'LL GIVE IT FIVE!"

SO, FOR THE FIRST TIME **FROST** MEETS HIS CHILDHOOD PIN-UP, JANETTE SCOTT.

EVER SINCE AT THE LOCAL **CARLTON CINEMA** HE SAW HER FIRST SCREEN KISS IN "NOW AND FOREVER", HE SAYS, "I FANCIED HER LIKE MAD."

NOVEMBER 1963. THE ASSASSINATION OF **PRESIDENT KENNEDY** INSPIRES A MOVING TRIBUTE FROM THE YOUNG **TW3** 'SATIRISTS'.

THEY ARE FÊTED IN **AMERICA** WHERE A RECORD OF THE SHOW BECOMES A BEST-SELLER.

FOR WRITING ONLY THREE LINES OF THE SCRIPT **FROST** SECURES A ROYALTY OF £2000.

JANUARY 1966. AT HIS LOWEST EBB **FROST** INVITES 17 CELEBRITIES TO A CHAMPAGNE BREAKFAST PARTY AT THE **CONNAUGHT HOTEL**.

THE GUESTS INCLUDE THE BISHOP OF WOOLWICH, LORD LONGFORD, NOVELIST **LEN DEIGHTON** AND THE **PRIME MINISTER, HAROLD WILSON**. WHY WERE THEY INVITED? WHY DID THEY ACCEPT? TO THIS DAY IT IS STILL A COMPLETE *MYSTERY!*

1966 **FROST** COMPERES A NEW PROGRAMME, THIS TIME FOR ITV. IT IS CALLED-**THE FROST PROGRAMME**. HIS BIG SCOOP IS AN INTERVIEW IAN SMITH.

"WHY ARE BLACK MEN DENIED PROMOTION IN THE RHODESIAN ARMY, NAVY AND AIRFORCE?" **FROST** ASKS.

"WE HAVE NO NAVY IN RHODESIA, MR FROST," REPLIES THE PREMIER

FROST HAS NEVER MARRIED. BUT HE HAS HAD MANY GIRL FRIENDS, THE FIRST BEING FILM STAR **JANETTE SCOTT**.

SHE STILL SPEAKS WITH AFFECTION OF HER FORMER LOVER - "BOOKS HE APPRECIATES GREATLY. WE USED TO HAVE GREAT FUN WITH BOOKS" SHE SAYS.

"IF HE WAS ENJOYING ONE, HE USED TO TEAR OUT THE PAGES AND HAND THEM OVER TO ME."

ANOTHER WOMAN IN **FROST'S** LIFE WAS **AMERICAN TV STAR SALLY STRUTHERS**

THEY MET IN **LONDON** IN 1973 AND DANCED THE NIGHT AWAY. MONTHS LATER **FROST** WAS IN **NEW YORK.**

BUT ROMANCE FADED. "HE PHONED MY MANAGER" **SALLY** SAID, "WHAT KIND OF A WAY WAS THAT TO GET HOLD OF ME? I WAS PROBABLY NO. 222 IN HIS LITTLE BLACK BOOK."

ACTRESS **JENNY LOGAN** STAYED WITH **FROST** LONGER THAN ANY OTHER WOMAN. "HE WAS A VERY SEXY LOVER," SHE SAID.

BUT **FROST'S** FRANTIC LIFE STYLE WAS TOO MUCH FOR **JENNY** IN THE END.

"HE ONCE WANTED ME TO FLY TO **INDIA** WITH HIM FOR THE DAY," SHE SAID.

AFTER **JENNY LOGAN** IN **FROST'S** LOVE LIFE CAME THE **AMERICAN FILM STAR CAROL LYNLEY**

"HE HAD A GREAT BIG EGO," SHE SAYS. "I LIKE THAT SORT OF MAN. "WE USED TO GO OFF WITH OTHER PEOPLE...

... AND THEN GET BACK TOGETHER AGAIN. BETWEEN US WE COVERED ABOUT 25 PEOPLE & ALL MUTUAL FRIENDS."

1970. **FROST** MEETS COLOURED **AMERICAN** SINGER **DIAHANN CARROLL.**

"SHE OF THE DELICATE FEATURES AND THE SMOULDERING TEMPERAMENT," IS THE WAY SHE IS DESCRIBED BY BURLY **AUSTRIAN** −BORN BIOGRAPHER **WILLI FRISCHAUER.**

THE TWO LOVERS BECOME ENGAGED. BUT AT THE LAST MINUTE **DIAHANN** OPTS INSTEAD FOR A BUSINESS TYCOON − **FREDDIE GLUSMAN.**

"It's his 1000th operation. . ."

Scott Case

Recluse tells of 'Night of Terror'

Goodman named by surprise witness

by Our Minehead Staff **Ted Thing, Barry O'Booze, Allbran Waugh, Donald Trelford** and a cast of thousands

A hushed courtroom was told today of a "night of terror", involving a negligee, a runaway motorcycle and a dead horse.

We apologise to readers that this picture of Sir Herbert Gussett cannot be printed owing to a dispute involving members of NOTSOBA and SODIT

Sir Herbert Gussett, giving evidence for the prosecution on the 49th day of the committal hearing in the Jeremy Thorpe case, was at times almost inaudible as he faced hostile questioning from Sir David Napoli, the Italian-born Soho restaurateur.

Sir Herbert told the court how, on the night of 23 April 1953, he had received a phone call from someone who gave his name as Lord Goodman.

"I was in bed at the time, dressed only in my pyjamas, when the phone went in the hall downstairs.

Horror

"I heard my housekeeper Mrs Tish answering the call. She was dressed only in a negligee at the time. I heard her say, 'there's no one called Bessell here – this is Sir Herbert Gussett's residence'.

"At this point I must have nodded off. I had a terrible nightmare about an enormous curly-haired bear jumping on top of me, catching me by the throat and saying, 'Everything is going to be all right – you are *sub judice*'."

Shock

Clenching his fists, and clearly near to tears, Sir Herbert sipped nervously at a glass of amber liquid before going on to describe how the nightmare figure slowly changed into the smiling embodiment of Lord Goodmanzee, the well-known London solicitor.

In his cross-examination, Sir David Napley shouted across the courtroom at Sir

Herbert: "I put it to you that everything you have said is a tissue of lies. You have dreamed the whole thing."

Gussett – "That is just what I was trying to explain."

Napley – "That may be. I put it to you that you are an inveterate lawyer, unable to distinguish fact from fiction."

Gussett – "That is perfectly true – I have a problem. I have had treatment. It was when I was staying with Dr Evil McKnievel, the GP and part-time stuntperson."

Napley – "Are you telling us that you are a sick man? No doubt you will soon be telling the court that you have been pursued all over the West Country by swarms of gigantic bees?"

Gussett – "Yes – they have tried to kill me on two occasions, once successfully."

Napley *(visibly brightening)* – "So you are, in a strictly legal sense, dead?"

Gussett – "That may well be the case."

Napley – "Is it or is it not the case that you have received an offer from the Watchett Parish Magazine for your memoirs?"

Gussett – "That is correct."

Napley – "They would not be interested in tittle-tattle about pink gins in the Officers' Mess at Jellallabad, would they? I put it to you, Sir Herbert, that Indian love-rites involving such figures as the Queen Mother, Zsa-Zsa Gabor and senior members of the Liberal Party would be more the kind of thing they would be looking for?"

Gussett – "Good thinking, sir. I will telephone the editor and put it to him right away."

Case in full . . pages 7-24

"Are we winning or losing? Can't focus this bloody telescope"